The Great Re-imagining

Spirituality in an Age of Apocalypse

The Great Re-imagining

Spirituality in an Age of Apocalypse

Theodore Richards

Little Bound Books
Small Books. Big Impact

HOMEBOUND PUBLICATIONS

Ensuring the mainstream isn't the only stream.

First Edition Paperback

ISBN 978-1-938846-94-6

Published by Homebound Publications and the Little Bound Books Chapbook Series

Front Cover Image © Tithi Luadthong | Shutterstock.com

Cover and Interior Designed by Leslie M. Browning

10 9 8 7 6 5 4 3 2 1

Also by Theodore Richards

Handprints on the Womb

Cosmosophia

The Crucifixion

The Conversions

Creatively Maladjusted

Dedication

For my wife, Arianne,
and my daughters,
Cosima, Calliope, and Vismaya

Contents

Preface

In November of 2016, long after I'd completed the manuscript of *The Great Re-imagining,* the American experiment with democracy ended. Or at least this looked like the beginning of the end. While the election of Donald Trump to arguably the most powerful political position in the world would seem rather fortuitous for a man who just wrote a book on the apocalypse, I really wasn't particularly happy about it. I would like to be able to claim I saw it coming, but the truth is I thought Trump would lose all along, even well into the night he was elected. I suppose I don't make much of a prophet of the apocalypse.

I don't mean to sound hyperbolic. After all, there are still plenty of functioning democratic institutions in the United States of America. But democracy requires an educated populace that can engage in a meaningful public dialogue. Donald Trump, the Twitter president, had revealed the complete failure of the most vital institutions upon which democracy depends: education and the media. Reality TV had replaced reality; Trump's tweets had replaced facts.

What I had indeed known all along is that things were coming to a head—and this book describes the ways in which we have reached the end of an old and failing worldview. We were confronted, as I suggest throughout this book, with a choice. The stories of the American democracy had become so muddled and confused with the narratives of white supremacy, of dogmatic neoliberal Capitalism, that a new story was required. Throughout this book, I have intimated ways in which the new story might bring forth a more vibrant, sustainable, just and compassionate civilization.

But there is no guarantee that apocalypse brings forth something better.

Trump's supporters felt something that was real: They saw that the American Dream was no longer viable; they felt the end of the American middle class and the erosion of genuine community; they understood, perhaps unconsciously, that the narratives upon which their identity rested were being challenged. But the American people chose fascism—fear and hatred of the other—over all the possibilities of a new world, a new dream. That's the thing about apocalypse: you can dive off the cliff into the unknown waters or you can cling in futility to the edge.

But there is a bright side. The truth is that whoever was elected in November was going to lead us over the same cliff. One side would have done so more gently, more slowly. But once you start over the cliff it doesn't much matter.

Is it possible that all the fear and anxiety over Trump's presidency is because it forces us to deal with things as they really are? We can no longer pretend that we don't have to deal with climate change or that technology will save us. We can no longer pretend we live in a post-racial society. We can no longer pretend that we haven't dumbed-down our society to such an extent that celebrity is more valued than substance.

We've got work to do.

* * * * *

Here on the south side of Chicago, I am confronted with another side of apocalypse. Here, we know that genocidal madness is a real possibility. Every time a young man is incarcerated or murdered by the police, ghosts of the past become present in the collective memory of the people. Black Lives Matter, the new rallying cry of this generation of activists, exposes the absurdity of our world and our times. Only in a crazy civilization would the assertion that one human life matters as much as another be controversial. Only in a crazy nation would tens of millions of people cast their votes in opposition to the winds of change—to "take our country back" from those who want their own liberation and equality. This is an apocalyptic moment.

We could see it coming with the Occupy Movement that began in New York. The economy was failing the masses. The very foundations of our civilization—the "free market"—were being challenged. The Occupy Movement wanted a revolution. It wanted an economy based on the principles of egalitarianism that most of our spiritual traditions claim to espouse.

At Standing Rock, the intersection of indigenous genocide and planetary ecocide brought about not merely a protest, but a movement. *We can't breathe!* was the cry of the urban masses, choked by toxic air and killer cops. It was in this spirit that the native peoples of North America rose up, too, confronting the confluence of government and corporate abuse that had been choking them for centuries. This is an apocalypse that brings together both Noah and the Book of Revelation, drowning and burning at once. With the oceans steadily rising, fires burned in the Appalachians and in the West. The Earth is on fire. The protesters there remind us that there is a different way of seeing the world, a wisdom that we've known for millennia.

But overcoming the capitalist order is no small task. Tens of millions of Americans chose the race baiting and scapegoating of a man who promised to return the jobs that they imagined were stolen by Mexicans, who told them climate change was a hoax, rather than a new vision of the world and a return to the wisdom of the indigenous peoples.

* * * * *

I do most of my writing from home. My daughters—ages eight, three, and one—are always around, playing and laughing, arguing and crying. Constantly making things. Constantly making and re-making worlds. Creating. Imagining.

There is an insanity, an absurdity, a hubris in this writing I do. I should shut up. I should just listen to them. They are teaching me what might be possible on the other side of the veil. The true opposite of fascism isn't going to be found in any political party. It is imagination. It is poetry. It is music. It is community.

Giving birth is a painful process. The apocalypse can be many things, but it will not be easy. What lies beyond the veil? Before we can answer that, we must learn again to listen.

–Theodore Richards
The South Side of Chicago, December 2016

Chapter 1
Apocalypse

THESE ARE THE END-TIMES. We hear this sentiment in one way or another from various sources. The Left tells us that imperialism and the colonial project that began five hundred years ago is coming to an end; the Right claims our society is unraveling as we lose our moral grounding. Scientists tell us that we are in the midst of the sixth mass extinction, ending the 65 million-year-old Cenozoic age; many Christians claim that Christ's return is imminent; and New Agers have claimed that 2012 or the dawning of the Age of Aquarius will usher in a new consciousness. Popular culture approaches this subject from all angles: from the evangelical millennialism of the *Left Behind* series to the literature of Cormac McCarthy to the ecologically-oriented Hollywood blockbuster *Avatar*. Unclear in all this is what exactly we mean by "the end."

The end means many different things to many different people. How we define the end has to do with how we define what exists here and now, what we believe to be real, what we value. It is a question, ultimately, of the sacred. Because an exploration in the end is a confrontation with that which—by definition—does not yet exist, what lies beyond the end can only be confronted through the imagination. While our values and beliefs about the quotidian, the mundane, define what we believe to be ending, what lies beyond is to be found only in our dreams.

* * * * *

This book is about the end—but it is not what you think. While I will draw from many sources that earnestly predicted that the complete and total end was imminent, I am making no such suggestion. Rather, I am suggesting that the Universe is repeatedly ending, in various ways: the phase changes of cosmic evolution; the evolutionary shifts that occur with mass extinctions and climate change; the historical transitions from one era to the next; the paradigm shifts that occur when human beings begin to think differently about who they are and their place in the Universe.

Apocalypse literally means revelation, referring to that which is revealed when an encounter is made with the temporal and spatial edge of the cosmos. Unlike other kinds of ends—the end of a political entity, for example—an apocalypse refers to an end that is *cosmic*. The ancient apocalyptic tradition, rooted in a particular cosmology and with certain cultural and scientific notions of how the Universe operates, held that the cosmos would end, ushering in an entirely new way of being. The reader may note—if you have not, you are not unlike most scholars on the subject—that an absolute end to the cosmos does not mean an absolute end altogether. For the souls, and even the bodies, of human beings continue to exist after this end occurs. So maybe it is not as much of an end as we suppose.

Just as an idea about the end-times is based upon a particular cosmology, so too is any form of spirituality. That is, one's worldview necessarily informs the way we understand the absolute and our relationship to it.

It determines the web of relationships in which we find our selves. Indeed, it determines how we understand not just the cosmos beyond, but the cosmos within—the Self, or psyche. And as that worldview falls apart, new forms of being human, new forms of spirituality, arise. This was the case during the axial age, when the great traditions we now think of as the "world religions" came into being. And it is the case now.

* * * * *

IN ORDER TO HAVE A DISCUSSION about this subject, it is important to clarify what is meant by certain key terms—and what *I* mean, because many of the terms I use in this book are contested and have multiple uses.

As stated above, apocalypse literally means "revelation". It refers to that which is revealed when an encounter is made with the edge. Partly arising out of the biblical prophetic tradition, the apocalyptic tradition differed from the prophetic in that it proposed not a transformation of a temporal, secular order, but complete transformation of the cosmic order. The apocalyptics no longer believed that the world's problems could be solved within the context of the cosmos they inhabited.

For them, the end of space and time—the edge of the cosmos, as it were—was the only way to redemption.

The apocalyptic tradition has come to be associated completely with the end-time, the study of which is called eschatology. Coming from the Greek *eskaton*, meaning edge or end, eschatology refers to that which lies beyond the current cosmic order, that which is so different from the way our current cosmos is structured that it can only be understood, or revealed, by a complete and total end.

To understand an encounter with the edge of the cosmos, one must reflect on the cosmology of a particular culture. A cosmology, or worldview—I will use these two terms interchangeably—refers to the basic assumptions and values made by a culture about reality, how it is ordered, and how the human being fits into it. The temporal end of the cosmos and an encounter with the edge of the cosmos can mean many different things depending on the cosmology of a culture. It is obvious, therefore, that any understanding of apocalypse requires a reflection on the cosmology out of which it arises.

Also important to bear in mind is that, just as the cosmos is that which contains and sustains us, provides us with our ultimate context, so too is a cosmology. The cosmos does so physically, whereas a cosmology does so spiritual and culturally. Modern scientists would tell us that the question of what lies beyond the cosmos is meaningless; for there is physically nothing else. Similarly, beyond a cosmology lies meaninglessness, for there is nothing else spiritually, nothing else that has value or meaning, nothing else that can be contextualized.

* * * * *

THERE ARE AS MANY WAYS TO UNDERSTAND the end as there are ways to imagine and represent existence—that is to say, there are infinite possibilities. The first, and most obvious, are ends brought about through catastrophe or through ecological change. Surely the dinosaurs experienced such an end 65 million years ago when the meteorite struck that ended their reign on Earth. Could they, in their dinosaur imagination, have been the first apocalyptics? I am inclined to say that apocalypticism is a peculiarly human phenomenon, but we can never know for sure.

Humans, of course, have encountered ecological collapse on various scales at many different times. While we generally think of the end as being a complete obliteration of the Earth, or even the Universe, it is important to remember that this is based upon our worldview. If an island is the entire world for a particular group of people, then the destruction of that island would be encountered as no less total than the destruction of the Earth—or its being rendered uninhabitable due to climate change—would be for modern humans.

One difference, I think, between the dinosaur and the human is that humans experience their world through culture. Because of our capacity for symbolic language, we create worldviews that give meaning to our world. It is impossible, therefore, to separate cultural or civilizational collapse from environmental, climatic, or even cosmic ones. The end of a way of life and the values associated with it can be experienced as an end no less total than if a meteor struck.

When the Nigerian author Chinua Achebe used the line from W.B. Yeats' poem the "Second Coming" for his classic novel *Things Fall Apart,* he was not using hyperbole:

> Turning and turning in the widening gyre
> The falcon cannot hear the falconer;
> Things fall apart; the centre cannot hold;

Mere anarchy is loosed upon the world,
The blood-dimmed tide is loosed,
  and everywhere
The ceremony of innocence is drowned;
The best lack all conviction, while the worst
Are full of passionate intensity.[1]

Achebe's work is about the effect of colonialism on a traditional African society; Yeats' poem was written in the aftermath of the First World War. This sense of unraveling, of chaos, of the loosening of that which once bound us together led both men to describe political and cultural disruption in cosmic terms.

* * * * *

Ends can be viewed in two different ways: as part of a cyclical pattern of death and rebirth, destruction and regeneration; or as a complete and total end that renders the cosmos in a permanent state of order and peace (or, perhaps, emptiness). While the apocalyptic tradition is generally considered to be the latter, it is worth considering both categories because they deal with similar experiences.

When considering the apocalypse of this moment one must also consider the very real effect of catastrophe and natural disasters. We are facing a moment in which the Earth may be dying. This is unheard of in human history. So, while this does not mean the end of the cosmos in its entirety, it is certainly a sort of end that is very real, very much related to the natural order, not just human perception.

But the apocalyptic tradition cannot be separated from human perception entirely, and the coming apocalypse is no different. While it may be true in an objective way that the Earth is dying, it is also true that we experience this destruction as an apocalypse because we are a part of the Earth and can scarcely imagine life beyond it. Similarly, we could experience the destruction of a civilization, a people, or a culture as an apocalypse if our identity is completely entwined with it. While dinosaurs could only experience one kind of apocalypse—the very real and literal catastrophe that led to their extinction—humans experience the end of a worldview as the end of the world, because our sense of self is cultural, symbolic, mythic.

In this last way, the end of a worldview *is* a cosmic end because a worldview—that is, a *cosmology*—is the context of human experience. It answers some of the most basic and essential questions for the individual in a culture: Who am I? What does it mean to be a human being? How am I a part of this world? When these questions can no longer be answered, the consequences are soul-shattering. This is not merely a psychological problem, for to shatter the soul is to shatter the cosmos. That is, the cosmos is not something "out there", but the intersection of human being, Universe and psyche.

But the apocalypse does not have to be something to be feared. In many traditions, it has been something that brings hope in the midst of terror, asking what is being revealed. And while many different answers to this question are found, it ultimately suggests that there is a possibility for a new way of being human. While this is generally described as something that happens beyond this world, that is because the transformation is so radical, the world so irrevocably transformed in the process, that it indeed appears to be—and in many ways is—a new world.

* * * * *

I am bringing a particular perspective and a specific agenda to this discussion. I believe that we are reaching the end. This observation is based not on an analysis of the ancient texts, nor will I provide exact dates. Rather, I am suggesting that the end is all around, if we can only perceive it. When Jesus speaks of it, he says:

> And when he was demanded of the Pharisees, when the kingdom of God should come, he answered them and said, "The kingdom of God comes not with observation: Neither shall they say, See here! or, see there! for behold, the kingdom of God is within you."[2]

The first words of Jesus in the earliest of the Gospels, Mark, are "The time has come, and the kingdom of God is at hand, repent, and believe in the good news."[3] While the English word "time" seems fairly straightforward, the Greeks actually had two words for time: *chronos*, referring the to normal flow of time with which the reader is surely familiar; and *kairos,* referring to a special time, a turning point, a unique moment in which a shift is occurring. It is this latter term that is used in the original Greek text.

Greek is not the only language that has more than one word for time. There are, in many cultures, multiple ways of understanding time. Although our culture seems to encourage a simplistic view of time, time is among the great mysteries of the Universe. Impossible to define, an awareness of time's passage affects our psyche like nothing else.

Jesus, in the above quotation, is suggesting that a cosmic shift is occurring—indeed, immediately before, when Jesus is baptized, the heavens part. The cosmos is shattering; a new way of being in the world is at hand. And what does Jesus tell us to do? Again, the English word is deceptive. "Repent" implies somehow that we are to blame for our current state. However, the Greek word used in the text is related to *metanoia*, calling upon us to transform our way of thinking, to change our hearts. With the cosmos shattering, the only option is for us to transform ourselves.

* * * * *

And what of the shift that is happening now? If the cosmos is indeed shattering, if we are indeed approaching an end, how should we transform our selves?

First, I should explain why I am choosing to interpret this particular moment as the end. The reader should recognize that I am not suggesting an absolute and total end of the cosmos, but a transformation from one cosmic phase to the next. This shift is not initiated by a deity from beyond the cosmos, but it is transcendent insofar as it comes from the human imagination—later, I will explain how this is an appropriate way to understand transcendence in light of modern science.

Part of my reason for interpreting this moment as apocalyptic has to do with the various crises that have arisen in recent years. Foremost among them is the ecological collapse that confronts us. Some will surely respond that at any moment there have been crises and to describe them as apocalyptic is to absolve our institutions of responsibility and human ingenuity of capability in solving them. While I do not wish to do so, I am suggesting that this moment is a crisis of a both a different magnitude and order. First, the magnitude of modern crisis reveals it as the first truly global crisis in human history. But even this does not make it apocalyptic in itself. This crisis is intimately linked with our way of perceiving the world. It is a crisis that has no institutional or technical solution. Only *metanoia*—on a cultural level—can save us.

Like Jesus, I am not primarily heralding the end of the old order and the birth of the new as a matter of prediction, but of prescription. We need to transform our selves. Neither Jesus nor I come to this discussion as a neutral observer. I am suggesting that we look at this moment as apocalyptic not as a way of avoiding the difficult work of solving our problems, but as a way to convey the urgency of the crisis, how radically our world will be transformed, and the depth of transformation required.

It cannot be ignored that I bring to this discussion an organic and intuitive relationship in addition to the intellectual. It is my intuition, based upon a life lived in the midst of it, that ours is a dying worldview. It mirrors the dying world in which species go extinct each day. And there is, of course, an intimate relationship between these two observations. They cannot be separate. Nor can my experience of it be separated from my analysis. The business of prediction is always problematic, so I will not claim to know the future. In fact, I rest quite comfortably with unpredictability. There is something I have always found quite limiting, even boring, about predicting the future. Part of life's mystery lies in our not knowing what lies ahead; part of life's beauty lies in our experience of the future as possibility rather than an unwavering line of determinism.

I bring also a particular sensibility to this discussion that I will describe as organic. Although the reader will find in this book a great deal of intellectual stimulation, I hope that I can also convey a sense that our challenge is not merely to think about our world and its problems, but to participate in it meaningfully and organically. This moment is apocalyptic not because we must come up with new ideas or, as a current advertisement suggests, "build a better planet" through technology, but that we must give birth to a new way of being. It is the act of giving birth that at once binds us to the most fundamental processes of the Universe as it has always been and allows us to arrive at something totally novel. It is in birthing that a new world is truly possible, that the transformation happening right now becomes cosmic, apocalyptic.

* * * * *

The coming apocalypse co-arises with an emergent cosmology that has not entirely been integrated into the culture. While most of us still think of the Universe as a great sphere, of time moving through space rather than as part of a space-time continuum, the notion of the edge in terms of what modern science reveals to us is actually far different from that of the ancient apocalyptic tradition.

The Universe is not a place but a process; and it is a process of differentiation in which new forms arise—life is autopoietic, "self-making", to the extent that it gives rise to forms that can adapt in ways that are harmonious with the community of life. The birthing process is only sustained to the extent that novel forms enter into communion. This is true biologically as well as psychologically. We cannot live in isolation.

So a dynamic tension always exists between our uniqueness and our need for community. The Universe reaches its end—apocalypse—when the individuation process comes to an absurd end, to a singularity that can no longer commune.

There is a theory that suggests that a Black Hole—a singularity—leads to a "White Hole", the birth of a new Universe. Just as our own Universe began as a singularity, it has been posited that every singularity gives rise to an alternate Universe. While it is impossible to verify this theory, we will explore its implications when we apply it to the psychic and mythic possibilities for this moment.

* * * * *

Apocalypse is fundamentally an expression of the human encounter with time. On an individual, personal, psychological level, our response to life is largely a response to a consciousness of time's passage. As we grow older, we become acutely aware of how fast our lives pass by. We relive our past, both in an interior way and in the outer choices we make. The past remains with us, lives in us, becomes more and more how we understand our world.

What is it about the past that is so seductive? Who has not been at least a little intrigued, if not mesmerized, at finding an old letter? In such moments, we remember the past, become the past, and in so doing, come to know our selves more deeply. This is to say nothing of ruins. For remnants of our shared past teach us not only what someone else did long ago, they reveal to us who we are. Pieces of that past remain alive in us even as, when we gaze out upon the stars, we know that a piece of one of those stars, long ago deceased and scattered throughout the heavens, lives on in our bodies.

My first encounter with the past in a conscious way was a summer spent excavating a cave in northern Spain, near Santander. Day after day we brushed aside dirt to find anything these ancient people might have to say to us. For in knowing them, even a little, we might, we supposed, come to know our selves.

But while our cave could offer only scraps, it was in Altamira that I entered the mind, the womb of our shared past. Only many years later did I read Picasso's response to Altamira: that everything since has been "decadence." Only years later did I reflect that this was not simply beautiful, but the birth of consciousness, the Universe waking up to itself in a completely new way. That this cave, in which people had painted their stories—stories of the handprints on the womb and of the profound relationship between predator and prey—was like seeing the inside of the human mind.

Years later, I crossed the Middle East, playing for hours in the ancient and empty cities of Bam (Iran) and Petra (Jordan). Being the only one in each of these incredible places, I rejoiced in the solitude. But it was something more than solitude that I found there. Perhaps, in realizing that something had ended here, I also perceived that we could not go back to those times. The days of the cave paintings are over. Even as the shamans created those masterpieces, they brought an end to the time before them, before culture.

But the effect of the empty past does not always come with the grandeur of Petra or the sublimity of Altamira. Several years after my journey across Asia, I found myself on an empty beach in Bahia, Brazil. An abandoned beach bar gave me respite from the sun, as I spent my time eating coconuts and playing in the waves. I wrote these words:

From our earliest days
The human has been the walking ape.
The ape that could stand straight
And swing her long legs
For days
Searching for nothing more
Than solitude.

Every wayfarer carries this memory
And every wanderer, bears the cross
Of the lonely oppression
Of a world too crowded
With walking apes

And not nearly enough room
For communion.

But there used to be a place
On the northern coast of Bahia
Where one could walk
Only a few miles from the town
Called Sitio do Conde
And sit on a beach
Alone
Under the ruins,
Of an old beach bar.

I went there to listen to the surf
And to hear the rhythm of the Earth
And Moon
Commune, with Yamaya.
To remember
The ocean
To remember
My wandering ancestors.

Only a few noises could be heard:
The surf

The wind
A lonely bird
And the faint sound in the distance
Of the mighty trucks
As they built the road
That would bring resorts
and tourists and money and crowds.

On the walls of the old bar
A graffito was written:
YANKEE GO HOME!
I stared at the sea
Unsure if I disagreed.[4]

Why I had come to this lonely beach was not entirely clear then, nor is it now. In a way, the past I sought mingled with a future; and that future was at once feared and embraced: I wanted the end to come, the promise of a future in which more lonely beaches could be found; but I feared that future in which roads bringing more tourists proliferated.

* * * * *

While the focus of the apocalypse is invariably the future, one cannot understand it without looking deeply at the past. Our experience of this moment and our expectations for the future—rightly or wrongly—are influenced by what we know about the past. To understand what is meant by apocalypse in the first place as well as how humans have experienced the end previously requires some study of the past, even if we intend to reinterpret the tradition in novel ways.

Moreover, one must not forget that the apocalyptic tradition deals not only with history, but also with a mythic past. In this book I will address both because I believe the lines between them are less rigid than is generally assumed, particularly in Modernity. The mythic past is frequently recapitulated in the apocalyptic future. That is to say, our imagination of an idealized past tends to predict our hopes for the future.

The possibilities for the future throughout history have been as varied as the cultures in which they were found. Always, in spite of our tendency toward determinism, the possibility of novelty is present.

* * * * *

While this book is not limited to the apocalyptic tradition in its assessment of the present situation, it would be impossible to understand our encounter with the end without understanding the ancient apocalyptic. We must first, however, understand what gives rise to the apocalyptic tradition.

The apocalyptic movement arose from groups of people who believed they were at the edge. While this was not a unique or new situation for humanity, the response was novel. That is, a new mythos arose that placed a special emphasis on the encounter with the edge in cosmic terms.

The apocalyptic tradition is rooted in three religious phenomena: the prophetic, the mystical, and the shamanic. It has been well documented that the prophetic tradition is the precursor to the apocalyptic among the Israelites. The prophets believed that God would intervene to bring about Earthly and political justice within the flow of history. The apocalyptic tradition introduced the notion that ultimate justice and salvation could only occur beyond this world—beyond the cosmos and the normal flow of time. It has been postulated that this had to do with the influence of Zoroastrian Persia. I do not doubt that this is true to some degree, but the Persian influence does not explain the ultimate origins of humanity's capacity to imagine a complete and total end to the cosmic order. It was the combined pressures of Roman Imperial power and Hellenistic culture that conspired to put the Israelite worldview under threat. The apocalypse did happen, of course, but not literally as predicted. Both Christianity and a re-imagined, Rabbinic Judaism were the results of these cultural and political pressures.

While anthropologists can surely find exceptions, the practice broadly known as shamanism is widespread enough throughout the world that I feel comfortable describing it as a nearly universal religious phenomenon. Shamanism arises in the context of an indigenous worldview, one in which the human relates to the world as a part of an interconnected web. The ecosystem provides the ultimate reference point, not the individual mind, for consciousness is embedded in nature and in the community. This community, which included the entire ecosystem but had a special place for the human, was understood in terms of a cosmology in which each individual understood her place in the world in relationship to the cosmos through myth. The myth conveyed to the individual an identity that could not be separated from the cosmos. The notion of something beyond the cosmos, therefore, was as nonsensical to this culture as it is to many modern scientists.

In many cultures, however, there were certain individuals who stood apart. These specialists—much like the artists of today—had the capacity for a consciousness that was less communal, more individual, than other members of the group. And their uniqueness gave them a unique capacity: they could separate their soul from their body and move beyond the cosmic sphere, giving them access to wisdom withheld from others. It was their role, therefore, to teach the people, to be the mythmakers, who, in shattering the barriers of the cosmos, could also shatter perceptions.

The possibility of transcendence was therefore born with the shaman. While there was not yet a sense of the cosmos having a finite, temporal end, humanity recognized the possibility of going beyond the cosmos—and going beyond a cosmology—through the shamanic journey.

But two more things had to happen before we could imagine an apocalypse: linear time and the alienation of the human from the traditional cosmology. Linear time comes into human conscious, at least in the Western tradition, largely through the Israelites. Their sense of themselves as arising within history, not as part of a repeating cycle, set the Israelites apart from the rest of the ancient world. For them, history involved unique events that had not happened before rather than the mere repetition of archetypal patterns.

Linear time cannot be entirely separated from the notion of individual consciousness. Among the Greeks, there began to arise a sense of the individual as separate from the collective. A disembodied, spiritual soul was what endured, not the collective, ethnic, or tribal identity. This is important because it forces the individual to deal with the issue of death. Adam and Eve did not start death; rather, their awareness of their individuality meant that they were no longer able to see themselves as enduring through the permanence of the cycles of nature of which they were a part. The Greeks dealt with the problem through the mystery cults, which led to mysticism, the union of the individual soul with the ultimate. This enabled the individual to transcend the body and the cosmos, to reach the edge of the cosmos. But, unlike the shaman who still considered time to be cyclical and the fate of the individual to be entwined with the collective and nature, the mystic had a temporal dimension. Mystics had answers for the fate of the individual after death.

* * * * *

We, like Christ after the *pneuma* enters him in Mark 1:15, are at the *kairos*, what Jung describes as "the right moment—for a 'metamorphosis of the gods', of the fundamental principles and symbols."[5] Such profound cosmic shifts are often described in eschatological terms. For both Jesus and the emergent Christians, the disruption of their cosmology and the imposition of a new culture led to a new religious worldview dominated by eschatological expectation. We are faced with a similar phase-change today at which some sort of "end-time" is imminent. Whether it is the end of life on Earth, the end of humanity, or the end of the modern, industrial worldview remains to be seen.

Particularly significant is the syncretism that existed both in the Hellenistic/Roman world and in the global economy today. Cultural, political, and economic imperialism typically leads to an intensified marginalization along with an increased exposure to new ideas, the combination of which can result in the emergence of a new worldview that seeks to subvert the established order. Disparate ideas influenced the historical Jesus of Nazareth and the way he was interpreted by early Christians, particularly in response to these pressures.

I am not arguing that Christian apolypticism is the answer to the planetary crisis. On the contrary, Christianity as we now have it, either dogmatically frozen in a context that no longer applies or distorted to take on the exact opposite of its original contextual meaning, cannot begin to address our current situation. But Christianity must be addressed for two reasons: first, it is the cultural context for the dominant imperial power, and ignoring it will only allow a distorted Christianity to dominate the unconscious; second, by exploring the ways in which Christianity responded to the transformative moment and subsequently transformed the world, we can figure out how to engage in a transformation today.

Central to the Christ myth is the notion of transformation as a response to crisis, injustice, and suffering. It is largely for this reason that the myth has been so appealing to so many for so long—suffering is an unavoidable part of life. Never properly dealt with, however, is how we can be transformed—"reborn"—in a way that does not lead to a dismissal of the real issues that face us in the world. Too often, eschatological expectation has been the context for rebirth. What we are faced with, however, is not the "end of time" but the end of our cosmology, the old worldview. Even in moments of real destruction—whether it is the temple or the biosphere—the cosmos remains. This turning away from the cosmos has a great deal to do with a turning away from the feminine and a fear of death. That is, we reject mother Earth because patriarchy has taught us that anything associated with her is sinful or corrupt; and in our fear of the knowledge that our bodies will die, we pretend that this embodied life in the natural, feminized world, is insignificant. In a healthy apocalypse, the eschatology will be *realized*, rebirth will occur both internally and within the cosmos, and we will embrace the feminine, the Earth, and death.

In many ways, the Hellenistic revolution parallels the conditions of today's world. The cultural syncretism of the Hellenistic world exists today on a global scale and a new cosmology is emerging that has no place in traditional religion. For some—the elites of the Hellenistic world then and of America now—these changes have brought greater opportunity and wealth. But today, no new religious, mythic framework has emerged to fit these changes, leaving all, even the rich, with a sort of psychic schism, a mythology that is inconsistent with the new information about the cosmos, and in the absence of an answer to the psychological problem of death, an existential crisis. In addition, the global economy has left certain groups of people feeling increasingly isolated and alienated. Many have been pushed toward fundamentalism as a response to the economic and cultural threat of Modernity. In the Hellenistic Age, one group that was particularly threatened by Hellenism was the Israelites.

The uniqueness of Israelite religion—the very foundation of which was constructed in contrast to the norm in the Near Eastern world—led to a unique response to the Hellenistic revolution. The predominant religion of the Near East was centered on the worship of a combination of male and female gods, recognizing the cyclical nature of time and the seasons upon which their agriculture depended. In contrast, the Israelites, who were pastoralists in their formative stage, developed a notion of time as linear, and a notion of themselves as emerging as a part of history—although there were some instances of an unconscious return to cyclical time—rather than honoring the cycle of seasons. Unlike their

Mesopotamian, Egyptian, or Assyrian counterparts, the Israelites believed that they emerged at a particular point in history. And because their connection to the divine, and to immortality, was to be found in the collective identity of Israel, the end of Israel meant total annihilation. The new threat of Hellenistic culture was resisted more fiercely in Israel than elsewhere, even as the means of resistance were the product of the Hellenistic Age.

* * * * *

There have been numerous examples of massive crises that led to a re-imagining of our selves, shifts, if not complete transformations, in the cosmologies, cultures, and spiritual lives of those who endured them. Easter Island stands out as perhaps the singular example—a warning, if you will—for the current planetary crisis. The decay and destruction of that culture was so complete when its resources were depleted that, because it is an island—much like our island planet—there was no coming back.

The Bubonic Plague, also known as the Black Death, killed perhaps one-third of the population of Europe in the middle of the 14th century. The aftermath of this calamity brought about both horror and possibility. Jews were blamed and massacred; war and chaos proliferated. At the same time, the Renaissance came in its wake. While this rebirth of ancient knowledge, lost to Europe for centuries, was the beginning of a brighter time, it also led to the fears, dualisms and pessimism that have become part and parcel of the Modern period: Prejudice against women and minorities intensified; the inequities and injustices of Capitalism and colonialism exploded onto the world. And it has never been the same.

In 1492, the Jews were expelled from Spain. The cultural flowering that had been Moorish Spain produced the classical period of Jewish mysticism, or Kabbalah. Some of the expelled found their way to a little mountain town in Palestine called Sefat. Led by Isaac Luria, this community would become the center of Jewish mysticism for years to come. Among the many contributions to mystical philosophy arising from Lurianic Kabbalah was the notion that our world was broken. Lurianic Kabbalah posited a cosmogony in which divine emanations could no longer be contained; the vessels that contained them were *broken*. In the aftermath of the expulsion, a cultural-historical disaster of unimaginable proportions, the Jewish mystics saw their world as broken, and their work to put it back together.

For several centuries, the trans-Atlantic slave trade ravaged Africa. For those who endured the Middle Passage, this was an apocalyptic event. Their experience was not merely one of agony and terror, but of the obliteration of a world, a way of life. The tragedy was a product of history in this sense: the magnitude and the form of the trans-Atlantic slave trade could only have occurred at the historical moment at which there was a confluence of economic, technological, and cultural forces that allowed it to happen. Whatever its causes, a grand experiment occurred in which various African peoples came together to create an entirely new culture. In North America, this flowered into the literary works of the Harlem Renaissance, the politics and theology of the Civil Rights Movement, Jazz, Hip Hop, and more.

The Axial Age is perhaps the most far-reaching example of a planetary shift in spirituality. During this time, there was a movement of the sacred from the mountaintop or the stream to the interior, the soul. This was the case for the Hellenistic philosophers, Vedantists and Taoist-Confucian sages alike. It transformed Judaism and Hinduism and gave rise to Christianity and Buddhism. All this came in the context of empire—and a rejection of the cooptation of tradition forms of religion by the imperial cult.

It could be argued that we are in the midst of another transformation, a transformation that requires us to take a step back to truly see. The Modern era brought with it a new, rational approach that turned religion into a private matter that contradicted the emerging scientific knowledge. Religion came to represent a purely psychologically endeavor. The world, in a sense, became disenchanted. We came to be alone, isolated, our primary pursuit, consumption, our primary identity, consumer. The axial religions, for many in the Modern world, simply had no meaning.

While I would argue that the world's religions still bring with them much of value—especially the mystics and the freedom fighters—it is also true that there is something new arising. The end of so many things carries with it a psychic end, the end of a mythos, a worldview, which invariably requires new forms of spiritual life. Indeed, it requires us to re-ask what it even means to be spiritual; it requires us to ask if there even is a god and what does god even mean in this new world; it requires us to re-imagine the sacred. It requires new stories.

How can we learn to live in this new, post-apocalyptic world? It is no coincidence that we have arrived at the end of our ability to perceive our place in the world as a part of an interconnected and meaningful cosmos at the same time that we have reached the end of our ability to live sustainably on the planet. The two are inextricably linked. There is no way we can live on the planet without seeing how we are a part of the planet, how we are connected to all. It is the failure to recognize this—the end of our spiritual lives, whether we are part of a religion or not—that has led us to crisis. But this is an opportunity as well. An apocalypse is an unveiling as well as an unraveling. In the chapters that follow, we will explore the emergent spirituality—that is, the ways in which we can reclaim our connection to the sacred, the absolute, the cosmic whole—in the context of the various emerging forms of human culture and life on the planet.

PART I

DEATH

Chapter 2
The Wild

> America, thought Adam, was savage because it could not abide the wild. He had come to see that he'd deeply repressed something wild in himself that he struggled to recover. So eager had he always been to reclaim his own humanity in the face of so many who would deny it that he... had unwittingly repressed the animator of his aliveness. The Wild.
>
> –*The Conversions*[6]

IN MY DREAMS THERE IS WILDNESS. One could say that there are two types of people—and I suppose what kind of person you are depends upon the civilization in which you come of age. Some dream of order. Mussolini would be a negative example of this type. In an Italy that had seldom been able to organize around anything—not even language—Il Duce created a political system, fascism, which cherished order above all else. Muhammad provides a more positive example, transforming the chaotic Arabian Peninsula into a coherent—and great—civilization through his holistic religious vision.

But I don't dream about organized states or religion. Having grown up in a civilization in which controlling the wild is one of our most cherished values—indeed, we have paved over most of the world in our fear of the wild—I dream of wild places. For some, such dreams are terrifying. For me, they are beautiful.

There is a balance between wildness and order—or chaos and cosmos, if you will—that any culture must find. Too much order leads to fascism; too much wildness means a descent into violence and anxiety.

Humanity has periodically encountered the wild in many contexts. We have always been a wandering species. We have tried to understand our world by constructing civilizations and creating cosmologies that allowed us to feel safe, to avoid the violence and anxiety to some degree. But it was always there. And always, there have been those among us who left the safety of civilized life behind, who stepped out into the wild. This story begins before we were really even humans, with the first apes who stood up and walked out onto the savannah.

My own country, the United States, was founded through an encounter with a land that was somewhat wilder than the Europe its founders knew, and far more wild in our own imagination. The worldview I have inherited—and rejected in my wild dreams—is the product of our encounter with and rejection of wildness. So much of the American imagination has been shaped by this encounter. With an evangelical fervor that was all too easy for this Protestant nation to adopt, we made it our mission to conquer the wild.

But what now? We have paved over the wild spaces, isolated the indigenous peoples, killed off most of the wolves and bears. Outer space is largely inaccessible. It seems that there is something in us that yearns for the wild again, something that needs the wildness even as we fear it. It seems that not only are the jungles and forests and bears wild; it seems that we are wild too. And we have paved over something in our selves.

My dream is of places where there are few people—no more than one person can know without losing the intimacy of true community—where there are open, unpaved spaces. My dream is not unlike the dreams of many of my ancestors. It is the dream of possibilities, the dream of re-embedding in the Earth and awakening the senses to allow the imagination to flow forth. This is my apocalypse.

The encounter with the wild is a quintessentially human experience. We were the apes who never lost our playful desire to encounter the edge; so, even as we repeatedly sought the Eden whence we came, we always also sought encounters with the wild beyond. The earliest people, in encountering the edge of their world, expressed this with the handprints they made on the walls of the caves.

These handprints were not unlike the handprints they must have seen on their own pregnant bellies. For they, like us, were encountering a future just as unknown to them as our world would be for the child in the womb.

* * * * *

Among the oldest stories of which there is a written record is the *Epic of Gilgamesh*. In it, Gilgamesh, the King of the ancient Mesopotamian city of Uruk, encounters the wild man, Enkidu. Gilgamesh—like humanity itself—is a man in between: part human and part god, approaching immortality but never quite attaining it. In Enkidu, he finds his greatest adversary and ultimate friend. For through him, Gilgamesh encounters something in himself that he'd nearly forgotten in his pursuit of the wealth and power of civilization: Wildness.

It is possible that, in Enkidu, we are encountering a memory of primordial wisdom that predates Gilgamesh's imperial civilization. Indigenous religion, as diverse as it is, has this much in common: it expresses the order of the cosmos in relation to the wild that lies just beyond the womb of human culture; and each—the cosmos and the chaos, culture and wildness—is necessary. Moreover, and particularly important at this moment in human history, indigenous spirituality tends to look at the world as inherently spiritual. That is, there is no clear distinction between the secular and spiritual worlds.

* * * * *

Ultimately, the axial traditions emerged as a way to reconcile the emerging imperial culture, less rooted in the local ecology, with the need to find the sacred in daily life—not merely in the temple of the imperial cult.

What happened during this period of human history is that the primordial cosmology became *interiorized*: each individual came to be considered a microcosm; the sacred center of the cosmos was now the human soul.

This brought with it both benefits and challenges. In a cosmopolitan culture, humans needed a way to find the divine in themselves. At the same time, in retrospect, one can see how this perhaps opened the door to a spirituality that would later remove the sacred from nature altogether. Indeed, early Gnostic and Manichaean traditions would be harbingers of the dead, inert Universe that would ultimately emerge in Modernity.

For the most part, however, pre-modern humans, whether they were a part of an axial tradition or an indigenous one, remained connected to the natural cycles of the Earth. One need not tell a traditional farmer about the value of wildness. Traditional farming has always recognized the benefits of maintaining a wild edge. This is where bio-diversity is maintained, and where soils can be replenished. When one looks at the practices of industrial farming and the depletion of our *soils*, we can see a parallel in the patterns of industrial culture and the depletion of *souls*. Cultivation was indeed one of the primary metaphors for spiritual growth in the axial traditions, born as they were in agricultural civilizations. Cultivation of the soul mirrored the cultivation of the earth.

It is in fact a major hallmark of the axial traditions that the cosmos came to be mirrored in the soul within. Through the wisdom of these traditions, we begin to see that, just as the wild is important in a healthy ecology, wildness is also important for a healthy soul. It is a strange paradox that while religion has been the lens through which the human makes order—cosmos—out of the world, religion is also marked by a certain degree of wildness, without which it becomes sterile. Simply look at how, in China, the wildness of Taoist philosophy balances Confucian order; or how the love-drunk ecstasy of Sufism balances the order of Islamic civilization; or how Jesus of Nazareth exhorted his followers to be like the birds of the air and the lilies of the field, breaking down sacred barriers in Israelite culture. Not enough wildness—too much order—breeds fascism. Sadly, our great religious traditions have often gone this route.

When despair for the world grows in me
and I wake in the night at the least sound
in fear of what my life and my children's lives may be,
I go and lie down where the wood drake
Rests in his beauty on the water,
and the great heron feeds.
I come into the peace of wild things
who do not tax their lives with forethought
of grief. I come into the presence of still water.
And I feel above me the day-blind stars
waiting with their light. For a time
I rest in the grace of the world, and am free.

–Wendell Berry, "The Peace of Wild Things"[7]

When cultivation becomes sterilization, nothing can grow. This is the great lesson we are learning in Modern agriculture, a lesson that is paralleled in Modern culture.

In only a few hundred years, since the onset of the industrial revolution, we have managed to destroy most of the planet's wild spaces. Most of us do not realize—perhaps because we have become so alienated from farms and farming—that the industrial revolution's impact on the way we grow food has been as significant as the proliferation of the factory and the automobile. Factory farms are now the source of most of the food we eat. Like other factories, they pollute the air and water; particularly problematic is the extent to which they are depleting our soils.

But this process could not be occurring without a deeper, spiritual process occurring alongside it. The Modern American school, designed to be like a factory—this is true not merely in the metaphorical sense, but in their very design—gives birth to the mentality that allows for the factory farm to exist. And the pursuit of wealth and growth at all costs, the religion of Capitalism, rationalizes the process, allowing for decent people to do terrible things in the name of profit.

Our alienation from the wild and textured world has relegated us to the two-dimensional. Lacking depth, we spend our time in front of screens, seeking after meaning and connection without touch, without awe, without wildness. A sterile, individualized spirituality has left our souls sterile. The great threat to humanity now is the sterility of soils and souls.

* * * * *

For Karl Jung, it was the shadow that provided the source of creativity. This is the unconscious part of our selves, the dark part. The Sufi tale of Mullah Nasruddin and the lost key demonstrates the significance of those dark places:

> Mullah Nasruddin was looking under a lamp-post one night. A man approached him, saying, "Mullah, what's wrong? Have you lost something?"
>
> "I have," said Mullah Nasruddin. So they began to look together.
>
> Minutes passed, then hours. Finally, the man turned to Mullah Nasruddin and said, "Mullah, we've been out here for hours. Are you sure you lost your key here?"
>
> "Well, no," answered the Mullah. "I actually lost it over there in that dark alley."
>
> Exasperated, the man responded, "Then why are we looking here?"
>
> "Isn't it obvious?" said Mullah Nasruddin. "This is where all the light is!"

The story demonstrates, among other things, our fear of the darkest parts of our selves. We remain with what's comfortable, ordered and presentable. But so much is lost when we fail to engage the darkness, the wildness, especially in our creative lives. The wildness within is connected to both darkness and chaos. On an individual level, we present an ordered version of our selves to the world. This is part of the reason that social media is so popular. The two-dimensional, Facebook version of ourselves is akin to what Mullah Nasruddin found under that lamppost: light shining on shallowness. On a civilizational level, we pave over those wild spaces. And in doing so, we pave over something wild in our selves.

And in the process, we have lost that wild and dark place in our selves that allows us to become artists. It is in confronting our uncontrollable and less-neat selves that we create something novel, both in form and in content. New stories emerge, which is the essence of art. There is a feedback loop at work on the planet: As we decrease the external wildness, we decrease our internal wildness, which inhibits our capacity to imagine and to create, which is exactly what we need to stop the destruction of the wild spaces on which the entire planet depends.

* * * * *

One could argue that there is no greater spiritual project in today's world than the reclamation the wild, a project paralleled by the ecological project to reclaim the wilderness. The two—the inner and the outer, the microcosm and the macrocosm—are inseparable. I have identified five reasons for them. Surely there are more.

The first, and perhaps most obvious, is that we are in the midst of an ecological crisis unparalleled in human history, largely caused by human behavior. The human relationship with the planet, of course, is determined by how we conceive of our selves. If we do not see our selves as a part of the earth, we remain apart. If we cannot value the wildness in our selves, we cannot value the wildness on the planet. Moreover, the loss of wild spaces worldwide is a major contributor to mass extinction and climate change.

Second, wild spaces teach us that we are at once smaller—because of the awesomeness of the cosmos—and larger—because we are interconnected—than the consumerist vision of the human allows. The Modern mythos that defines the human conflates our identity with the brands we can buy. We are consumers. In spite of the bravado of Modern hubris, we actually suffer just as much from a shrunken-down vision of the human. We fail to realize that, as part of an interconnected web, we are a part of a larger, more awesome whole than anything offered on the television screen. It is the very multi-dimensionality of wild spaces that allow for this sense of awe, of aliveness, so absent on the screen.

Third, wild spaces allow us to get in touch with our own wildness, and wildness is where creativity comes from. This creativity, evidenced as far back as the cave paintings, is what makes us human.

Fourth, wildness teaches us the value of diversity. There is a practical value in this. Without diversity, we lack the capacity to find new solutions. In an organism, a lack of genetic diversity can mean an inability to deal with new diseases. In an ecosystem, a lack of biodiversity can mean death. Modern monoculture has put the planet at risk; we have no solutions other than the clearly unsustainable ideas of industrial Capitalism.

Fifth, wildness is beautiful. This has value for its own sake—indeed, valuing it at all means letting go of the tyranny of utilitarianism that denies that things can have value without a practical use.

I don't know exactly what a prayer is.
I do know how to pay attention, how to fall down
into the grass, how to kneel down in the grass,
how to be idle and blessed, how to stroll through
the fields,
which is what I have been doing all day.
Tell me, what else should I have done?
Doesn't everything die at last, and too soon?
Tell me, what is it you plan to do
with your one wild and precious life?

–Mary Oliver, "The Summer Day"[8]

So what, then, does a new spirituality of wildness look like? This, of course, is not for me, or anyone, to prescribe. But I can say that it would involve being outside more than inside; that it will involve the creative energies that wildness fosters; that it will involve new—and also very old—ways of growing food; that it will recognize our interconnectedness as opposed to our individualism. In the end, a spirituality of wildness will help us to see that it is not only the church or the temple that's sacred—it all is.

Chapter 3

Spirituality in the Age of Climate Change

Apocalypse presents us with a choice. Often, this comes in the form of an over-simplified, fork-in-the-road choice, a black-and-white depiction of a world far grayer and more complex than our narratives indicate. At the same time, there are indeed choices we face at this moment that can be accurately depicted in this way, for Modern life has given us the delusion that we can have it all, that we can, for example, continue to live our bloated, Western lifestyles and not steal from our descendants or from the world's poor. Indeed, the ancients, in their acute understanding of the stark choices with which nature presented them—Modernity has largely obscured this—have much to teach us.

* * * * *

We live in an age of destruction. This cannot be avoided. The newspapers are filled with data about climate change. And while there is some value in the data, all the information seems to lead to very little change. In fact, one could argue that the tyranny of data, the over-stimulation of a particular type of knowing coupled with the under-stimulation of all the other senses, leads us further and further down a path of destruction. What is needed, in part, is the opportunity to embrace the spiritual work of despair, to look at the dying seas and the disappearing animals in the face and suffer with. Compassion, that most fundamental of spiritual principles, is not merely about being kind; it is also about suffering with another—even, ultimately, suffering to the point that we no longer can make a distinction between self and other. This is the work of deep ecology, work that, in the age of climate change, brings with it profound suffering and requires a radically re-imagined spirituality, a radically re-imagined human identity.

* * * * *

Once, I traveled around the world, largely overland. I traveled by foot, bus and train. I hitchhiked, rode on the back of flatbed trucks and motorcycles. I passed through languages and peoples and bioregions foreign to me, through the Buddhist realms of the East, through the Indian subcontinent, the Islamic world. It was only the beginnings of the Internet age, so I had no smart phone; there was no wifi. I was, for much of the trip, deeply disconnected. But in the end, when I arrived back in Chicago after a year away, I had done something not only privileged, but also something that separated the age in which I lived and me from most of my ancestors. I had experienced our planet as a sphere. While I hadn't gone into space to see it as a little blue island, I could feel that the planet of which I am a part, from which there is no escape, was round, and finite.

And because I did not merely fly from one wealthy, Westernized city to the next, I also saw the suffering. The shantytowns of impoverished megacities. The dried up rivers. The malnourished and the filthy. The coughing, constantly, in the polluted air. To circumnavigate the globe is to see a planet in despair, from which there is no escape.

* * * * *

The Earth is something like a macrocosm. It represents a whole that functions as the entire world, and within it wholes that function as worlds—ecosystems. The ecosystem is the basic context for life. Every human story about who we are and our place in the world necessarily began with ecology. And while an ecosystem functions as a closed system, it can only momentarily escape the reality of its larger context, just as the Earth cannot escape its cosmic context, and is confronted, from time to time, with things like the rock that killed off the dinosaurs. Ecosystems *seek* equilibrium. That is to say they are in constant flux, and small fluctuations can lead to greater, and sometimes fatal, imbalances.

The introduction of a new species, variances in temperature or rainfall, disease—all these can lead to an ecological collapse. And, because the ecosystem is the basic context for life on the planet, ecological collapse is apocalyptic in scale. The human, however, seems to have the imaginative capacity to delude itself into the belief that life is possible beyond ecology. Ironically, this is the capacity that we have associated so often with our salvation; but perhaps it is our demise.

* * * * *

It has been frequently suggested that technology will solve the ecological crisis. While this is probably inaccurate, my concern is not chiefly accuracy, but the underlying psychology that such an approach suggests. For to suggest that technology will provide a solution to the ecological crisis reveals that we are a culture incapable of sacrifice, that rather than changing our lifestyles, we are hoping that some kind of technological savior will swoop in and allow us the use of our cars, our steaks from Argentina, our green lawns in the desert.

The reality of our situation is somewhat different. While technology will improve, allowing us to retain more of our current lifestyle than would be possible, the reality is that we are so far from living sustainably that no technological improvement could possibly allow the entire planet to live the Western, middle class life style without destroying the biosphere.

The reader may notice that I have said "the entire planet," not merely the privileged Westerners who live this lifestyle today. And this brings us to the crux of today's moral dilemma, the crossroads at which we find our selves. Just as industrial Capitalism has created conditions under which the wealth of a few depend on the suffering of the many, global industrial Capitalism relies on this not merely due to the rules governing the capitalist system, but also because of the fundamental ecological realities of our planet.

* * * * *

A RECENT STUDY SPONSORED BY NASA's Goddard Space Flight Center warns that global industrial civilization could face imminent collapse in the coming decades due to unsustainable resource exploitation and increasingly unequal wealth distribution.[9] The study points out that although we have grown accustomed to thinking of permanent growth as the norm, human history is filled with cycles of growth and collapse.

> The fall of the Roman Empire, and the equally (if not more) advanced Han, Mauryan, and Gupta Empires, as well as so many advanced Mesopotamian Empires, are all testimony to the fact that advanced, sophisticated, complex, and creative civilizations can be both fragile and impermanent.[10]

The study further refutes the notion that technology will solve all of our problems.

> Technological change can raise the efficiency of resource use, but it also tends to raise both per capita resource consumption and the scale of resource extraction, so that, absent policy effects, the increases in consumption often compensate for the increased efficiency of resource use.[11]

Improvements in technology tend only to allow the elite to consume more resources, which solves nothing. So, first, we must recognize the interconnectedness of ecological and economic justice. Second, we must address the deeper, spiritual crisis: as long as we find value and meaning only in consumption, we are headed for unavoidable planetary collapse.

* * * * *

The choice we have is at once simple and complex, local and global, impossible to imagine and so clear and attainable it will one day seem impossible to imagine that we had so much trouble reaching it. But what is the trouble? Why, if our scientists tell us that we will destroy ourselves if we do not change, do we fail to change? (Those who claim not to trust scientists are usually either disingenuous or lying to themselves; after all, we all seem to trust scientists when it comes to any other aspect of our lives). Why would we even have to give it any thought? The answer has to do with our mythology—the stories we tell ourselves about who we are. We have told ourselves that we are separate from nature and have a spirituality that reflects this. What, then, does a new spirituality to facilitate the passage—a shared, planetary rite of passage or shamanic journey—to the other side of ecological crisis? I believe that our spiritual lives must be re-imagined to honor three areas of human fulfillment that have long been neglected: (1) diversity; (2) simplicity; and (3) interconnectedness.

* * * * *

DIVERSITY IS A WORD WE HEAR ALL THE TIME. Generally, in our society, it is considered a "good" thing, perhaps even a "value", particularly among liberals. But little more is said of it than that we should appreciate diversity because it makes for a more interesting culture and because—in the name of "tolerance"—we should not ostracize those who are different. While I agree with these sentiments, I'd like to make an argument for diversity that speaks to the very survival of humanity, an argument rooted in biology and, in this case, applied to the world's great spiritual and cultural traditions.

The current ecological crisis has brought the term biodiversity into the public sphere. Most of us, regardless of educational levels, recognize that a lack of biodiversity—that is, fewer varieties of living species—is a catastrophe in the midst of an ecological collapse and a mass extinction. This presents a problem in two ways that relate directly to cultural diversity. First, the loss of biodiversity leaves gaps in ecosystems when certain niches are no longer filled. We need a predator like a wolf, for example, because that niche has repercussions throughout an ecosystem. Without the wolf, species it preys on become too abundant, leading to the destruction of other species, and so on and so on.

It is worth pointing out that our destruction of these predators arises out of deeply ingrained fears. The wolf, the polar bear, the great cats of the African plain—these represent fears we have held for millennia.

They represent the wild. As mentioned in chapter 2, to destroy the wild beyond is to destroy something wild in our selves; in paving over the world, we have paved over our own souls. And we are only beginning to recognize how deeply interconnected are the inner and the outer, the soul and the cosmos.

A culture, like the ecosystem, requires a diversity of thought to provide a similar balance. When all information is passed on through the corporate media, it is extremely difficult for dissenting or novel views to be heard. This is a problem not merely because it marginalizes certain kinds of thinking, but also because that marginalization threatens our survival. When the only ideas that our politicians have to deal with the ecological collapse are technology and the market, we are in deep trouble. When the only idea our educators can come up with for the next generation is more testing, we risk perpetuating a cycle of absent imagination—and it is imagination that we most need at this moment.

Second, a loss of genetic diversity in a species leads to a loss of possibilities for that species' survival. Factory farming, for example, leads to a narrowing of the genetic make up of the species we consume. The many breeds of cows that arose through animal husbandry were an expression of the unique circumstances and ecologies in which those animals evolved. Today, we only favor breeds that can survive in the horrific industrial conditions of the factory farm and that produce large quantities of milk. There are many problems with the approach, but I will focus here on its consequences for the survival of the species. This narrowing, in the event that climate conditions change or a new disease is introduced, makes it far less likely that the species will find an evolutionary solution for survival.

A loss of cultural diversity can have a similar result. The imposition of Western industrial culture on the rest of the world through globalization marginalizes many of the world's great religious traditions. Indeed, even those who profess to be strict adherents to a particular faith have lost elements of their tradition in subtle ways. How much do Islamic fundamentalists know of Ibn 'Arabi? How much do Christian fundamentalists know of Thomas Aquinas? A superficial diversity in which there exists a shallow "tolerance" for various faiths is not enough, either. A species in crisis requires radical ways of looking at the world. Moreover, if we take the lessons of ecology to heart, the sort of interfaith approach that waters down every religion to a sterile and perfunctory sameness misses the opportunity for the diversity of ideas required in the face of the unknown.

The loss of languages that parallels the loss of biodiversity is a good example of how we are losing cultural diversity. Each language represents a completely unique and not-entirely-translatable form of wisdom. Like a species, it arises in a particular context—in the case of languages, this context is both ecological and cultural. Once lost, like a species, it can never be recovered. If everyone speaks only English, we only have one way of understanding our world.

A consequence of the loss of biodiversity can be found in genetic engineering, which can lead to the quick extinction of a species due to the presence of a "Trojan gene"—that is, a gene created for a trait that serves industrial farming but, when introduced to the general population, leads to its demise. Similarly, a sort of Trojan idea—in this case, that we are primarily isolated individuals, consumers, and two-dimensional Facebook pages—which allows us to live in the sterility of Modern industrial culture and which leads us to become increasingly passive consumers rather than creators of culture, can lead to the demise of our species as many of the common assumptions and conveniences of Modernity unravel.

If religion has any role in the future of our species, we must find a way to retain its diversity in the face of globalization. Indeed, the diversity of our religious traditions is perhaps one of their greatest values in the face of an uncertain future.

* * * * *

In addition to diversity, simplicity is a spiritual value that must be reclaimed in the age of climate change. Sadly, much of the growth in religion is in the spirituality of prosperity. The prosperity gospel, which holds that God's favor is demonstrated through material wealth, predominates in our growing megachurches. Tellingly, New Age spirituality has its own version of the prosperity gospel in such best selling books and videos as *The Secret*, which tells its followers that it is one's mind and belief that leads to riches. It doesn't take much to see that one must only replace "mind" with "God" and we have essentially the same thing: capitalist, materialist spirituality. In truth, the only one getting rich is the pastor at the megachurch and the writers of books like *The Secret*. And they represent a dangerous perversion of the traditions they claim to uphold. How could we get further from the gospels, which celebrate simplicity and poverty and rebuke material wealth, than the prosperity gospel? The New Age ideas that claim to be based on Eastern or esoteric traditions are equally distorted.

In each case, one obvious failing of this philosophy is that it cannot recognize how we are all in this together. Climate change can indeed be overcome with a change of the heart and mind, but in exactly the opposite of the way that the prosperity gospel suggests. For there is no individual wealth in an age of climate change. We are all on a sinking ship together.

What many spiritual traditions have offered is a way to value simplicity. Just look at our monastic traditions, for example, in the East as well as the West. The voluntary simplicity of many of these traditions taught that a good life was not found in material wealth, but in mindfulness and in beauty. It was found in being connected and in doing good and kind things to others. It was found in purposefulness. All this, with the rejection of consumption, was the spiritual practice of simplicity. It required not merely a change in lifestyle, but a change in values. Stories abound—from Gautama in India to Francis in Assisi—of spiritual teachers who had great wealth but rejected it. It is now a time to reject our collective wealth in the Western world, and to return to a simpler lifestyle.

* * * * *

The question still lingers, however, as to why one might do such a thing. There are many reasons for the rejection of Capitalist consumption. But I would suggest that the spiritual answer lies somewhere around the notion of interconnectedness, a completely new—and again, very old—way of seeing our selves.

Indigenous traditions have always seen themselves as part of an interconnected whole. So there is nothing new in seeing oneself this way. It is, in fact, the way most humans would have understood themselves for almost all of our existence on the planet—as embedded in an interconnected ecosystem. This would have been true to such an extent that concepts such as "ecosystem" and "nature" are entirely Modern constructions. That is, it is in our separation from nature that we even began to notice it was there. But then, we largely began to see it as a resource. The indigenous worldview is one that sees a far less rigid distinction between the self and the other members of one's community and ecology. The people and the ecosystem were the cosmos, and each human the microcosm of that cosmos.

It should be pointed out that there are tremendous differences between the indigenous lifestyle and our own. One cannot, I believe, simply adopt an indigenous worldview while driving our SUVs around and getting our food from the supermarket. In addition to the lifestyle difference, there are also differences in the magnitude of our conception of world. We no longer have the felt sense of belonging to a particular part of the forest. We are a planetary species, and most of us, on some level, feel ourselves to be planetary beings. It feels nearly impossible to fully embrace an indigenous consciousness in Modernity.

There are also, embedded in all the world's religions, vestiges of this indigenous worldview. The notion of self—or rather, no self (*anatman*)—in Buddhism, is a primary example. For the Buddhist, the concrete, unchanging Self is the ultimate attachment, the ultimate illusion. It is not that we don't exist; it is that we are nothing but relationship. Profoundly interconnected, we only exist as a web of relationships. There is no better model for an ecological spirituality than this.

* * * * *

It is undeniable, however, that the Modern human feels a certain separation from nature. We see our selves as individuals, which brings with it both freedom and loneliness. The true path to an ecological spirituality lies not in a return to an imagined past but in re-imagining our future. That is, how can one be at once aware of the uniqueness of the human and human consciousness and, at the same time, deeply connected and embedded in nature? This is part and parcel of what Thomas Berry called our Great Work, and it requires both an intellectual understanding of the relational nature of eco-system, Earth, and cosmos, as well as what I will call, borrowing from David Abram,[12] the *sensuous*, an awakening of senses, emotions and body to discover and rediscover our place in the Earth community. This place can be at once unique and, at the same time, no different from that of the oak tree, the lion, or the butterfly. It is no different, even, from the bacterium or the horse fly.

Just as the powerful illusion of our separation from nature led to the absurd decision to destroy our only home, it is only through the spiritual awakening of the sensuous that we can make a different choice, for life.

Chapter 4
The End of Capitalism

THE NEW ECONOMY HAD TO BE EMBODIED, value had to be expressed and experienced as the sensuous. The problem he had, as he sniffed the sea and rode in darkness towards a possible death, was that he had no words for this economy. For every word he uttered seemed to occupy some non-spatial space, a place that existed only in the mind. Words referring only to other words, just as in finance money made money, without any bodily-experienced product. In darkness, he reflected on his great mission: to find words—was it poetry he was after?—that could actually only be spoken from a body. In darkness, he understood that in the economy upon which he'd built his career was an economy without *oikos*. Without the body to share in the process of production, it was as if the world had disappeared.

–*The Conversions*[13]

Since the end of the Cold War, there has been a consensus among the political and media mainstream that "There Is No Alternative" to Capitalism, particularly the form of Capitalism one finds in the context of globalization. "The Free Market", it is said, will solve all our problems, and become the organizing principle the world over. The conflation of Capitalism and freedom itself has muted any debate that would suggest otherwise. At the same time, recent economic crises coupled with a growing clarity that unlimited growth is destroying the biosphere may suggest that the Capitalist era is coming to an end.

To understand this, we have to find a little bit of clarity about what Capitalism is and how it has come to dominate the planet. At its core, Capitalism is less about a free market than it is driven by systems of debt and corporatism for growth and expansion. Its roots lie in colonialism, an era in which indebted corporations and governments used the power of the gun to extract resources and exploit peoples ("markets") around the world. Capitalism breeds an insatiable need to expand and grow—consequently it requires a *cosmology of consumption*: a culture that understands the human being as primarily deriving meaning through what it can buy.

But where does this need for expansion lead when there are no more nations to conquer? Where does this lead on a spherical planet with finite resources? It would appear that we have reached the end of Capitalism.

* * * * *

Capital has responded in two ways to its imminent demise. First, Capitalism requires us to ignore the reality of climate change. This is done by either by denying it outright or by pretending it will be solved by technology—even though all the evidence suggests that improvements in technology only lead to more consumption. This is because we are not only living in a Capitalist economic system, but within a Capitalist worldview. Capitalism should perhaps be studied not merely as an economic system, but also as a system of belief; it is properly understood through the lens of theology rather than science.

Second, the end of new markets to exploit leads to increases in privatization and in wars to create new markets. The wars will be justified as in the name of freedom; the privatizations will be done in the name of efficiency. Both are lies. When the commons are privatized, it is done to make money by creating new markets. And when education or healthcare is privatized they become about profit rather than learning or healing. It also means that we lose our public, shared spaces. We become isolated, atomized.

The consequences for this are clear: the destruction of the biosphere; the destruction of human culture that can only be fostered and thrive in shared, democratic space; and the destruction of our interior lives as we understand ourselves primarily as consumers.

* * * * *

Centuries ago, a revolution occurred in response to the Western world's most powerful institution allowing people to buy the forgiveness of sins–"indulgences". Martin Luther's famous response, coupled with a radical change in the way information was spread by the printing press, changed Western culture irrevocably. The Supreme Court, arguably the Western world's most powerful institution today, has again allowed the purchasing of sins. We call the mechanism of this purchase "the corporation". Because it is recognized as a legal "person" but cannot be held accountable as one, and because the corporation has far more wealth than most individuals, the corporation is able to exercise disproportionate influence on the American political system. Politicians are paid off by the corporation to allow them to indulge in various sins from ecological destruction to contracts for prisons and weapons to the denial of health benefits and working wages.[14]

As a result of the powerful influence on our political system by the corporation, we are in the midst of an unprecedented period of "deregulation". The market has been transformed in myriad ways that benefit the wealthy. While the direct causes for this are complex and varied, it has one simple root: a theology that conflates wealth and merit, poverty and sinfulness.

There are two basic and profound fallacies promoted in the popular discourse, assumptions that have allowed for a Right-Wing ideological bias to dominate any discussion of economic policy: First, the false dichotomy between the "free" market and regulation; second, the conflation of wealth and goodness, bringing about the desire to punish the poor. As a result we find ourselves in the midst of four decades of Right-Wing policies—coming from both political parties in the United States—that have resulted in a shrunken middle class, a greater proportion of wealth for the super-rich and unprecedented and unchecked ecological devastation. The markets will correct these problems, we are told, as if that would be any consolation for our grandchildren born in uninhabitable ecosystems.

While presented as "rational", this faith in "the market" is just that—faith. It is the product of the theological position, particularly powerful in the Calvinist branch of Protestantism that provides a basic context for American culture, which considers poverty to be something like a punishment for sinfulness. Indeed, while it reaches its nadir in Calvinist theology, the connection between debt and sin goes all the way back to the times of Jesus. Trapped in a cycle of debt and poverty out of which they could not escape, the Israelites were told, under the Romans, that this debt-sin (the same word was used for both) was owed to the Roman authorities just as the sacrifice was owed to the Temple authorities. How ironic it is that Jesus (yes, the same Jesus whose name we hear on the lips of every Right Wing politician) offered an alternative: a forgiveness of debt.

It has long puzzled many on the American Left how

politicians like Paul Ryan and their voters could purport to be devout Christians while advocating economic policies closer to the atheist Ayn Rand than the Jesus of the gospels. The cynical position that politicians are knowingly appropriating Christianity is only part of the story. For the American Religious Right, the punishment of the poor is held as a theological position no less important than the resurrection.

The economic position of the Republican Party today is based upon a two-fold obsession: the punishment of the poor to appease their own guilt and the removal of the government's debt as a means of punishment. Neither is based on sound economic policy; both arise out of theological assumptions. That is to say that the Tea Party fixation with a balanced budget—while purported to be about responsible financial management—is the product of this theological position of sin and punishment. While there is some truth in the notion that the government wastes money and overspends, very few on the Right are serious about fixing the problem of waste: if they were, they would be willing to cut defense spending. The solutions on the Right are more about punishing the poor for their poverty, for their debt—"entitlements"—are the root of this government evil, the story goes.

Freedom, or the free market, is always found through the imposition of certain rules that allow for the greatest freedom within those parameters. Neoliberalism and Libertarianism are fantasies: Only the anarchist truly believes in a de-regulated economy. Neoliberalism wants its rules to benefit the American industrialist, or corporate farmer, or financier; the libertarian, of course, wants the government to protect those who have the capital. American Libertarianism's roots can be found in the desire to be "free" to steal land from the indigenous peoples and to steal the bodies of Black people. Both Neoliberals and Libertarians advocate myriad government controls and regulations to benefit the wealthy. Neither would advocate the truly unregulated space in which the poor could simply rise up and take what the wealthy have. The truth is that markets function best—indeed, they are the freest—when they can be created and cultivated and guarded against unfair practices. Not only are markets always subject to a certain amount of regulation—that is, the market is a space that is constructed by society in which to trade—but the lessening of regulation in the market invariably leads to the increase of control in other areas, namely the penal system. The illusion of a market that is somehow free and natural leads both a less egalitarian society and, perhaps more significantly, the belief that the poor are outside of this natural order and must be punished. The ascension of Chicago School economic policy in the United States has been coupled not only with a shrinking middle class but also with unprecedented mass incarceration.

* * * * *

There are few events in human history that so severed people from their historical, ecological and cultural contexts like the Middle Passage. American slavery was hardly unique in its enslavement of people. But the immensity of the Middle Passage and the subsequent racialization of the Africans in the New World made the break from their previous culture unimaginably severe. It was a severance of apocalyptic proportions. New stories were required; the imagination of the enslaved Africans would be their salvation.

To understand the immensity of the task of re-making a world, one must consider the completeness with which American slavery—and this is what made American slavery so uniquely brutal—eradicated the worldview of the enslaved. This began with racializing them. That is, the slaves would henceforth be identified primarily by their racial caste. There was no possibility of full humanness for an African American in this system. They lost their names, their language—everything that gave their world meaning. Even family structure was disturbed by this system.

Ironically, and not without controversy for some who would consider it to be the religion of the oppressor, a major way for the disparate groups who would come to be known as African Americans to deal with oppression—and to re-constitute their world—would be Christianity. Introduced to them by the radically egalitarian evangelical movement known as The First Great Awakening, the slaves saw quickly that the stories of the Bible were *their* stories. They were stories of a people enslaved seeking freedom; stories of a people disinherited seeking their rights; stories of a people pushed to the margins seeking their humanity. It was an act of collective, creative genius: to take the stories of their oppressors and turn them into stories of their own salvation.

The Bible is a complex and inconsistent text. It has been used to justify racism and equality, slavery and freedom, Capitalism and socialism, freedom fighters and colonists. That said, it is also true that if one steps back and takes the broader view, the major themes are clear. Sometimes, however, it takes the clarity of the outsider—the wisdom of the margins—to perceive the obvious. To the slaves, the Old Testament was a story of a people who were enslaved and found freedom in the Promised Land. The New Testament was a story of a man offering the possibility of freedom by re-imagining the sacred and breaking the psychic barriers that divide us. *Freedom.* It was the word that would have meant the most to an enslaved people. Salvation could only be understood in those terms.

For Jesus, the "disinherited", to use Howard Thurman's term, were the Jews of Palestine who faced economic, political and cultural oppression. In particular, it must be understood that Jesus not only was a member of a group who faced political oppression from Rome and cultural hegemony from the broader Hellenistic world, he was also near the bottom of that group economically. While the language of the synoptic gospels is not completely explicit about this, it is clear that his method of storytelling and his apocalyptic imagination is that of a man from the margins, from the bottom. His Kingdom of God turned this world upside down, eradicating the barriers that excluded him and his people. This was not at all obvious to the plantation owner; but it was obvious to the slave.

Jesus came from a tradition of the wisdom of the underclass. As a day laborer, he talked and broke bread with men who were barely scraping by, who were trapped in cycles of debt, who feared for their freedom and the sustenance of their families. The slave who heard the Sermon on the Mount would have heard the same yearnings Jesus felt.

Who, then, is today's underclass? Who are the disinherited who could understand the perspective of Jesus most clearly? As in the time of Jesus, the issues of class and economic justice cannot be entirely isolated from other issues such as race, ethnicity, politics and, of course, ecology. But we will first identify three core groups who are marginalized due to economic conditions today.

* * * * *

The first group refers largely to the political, social and economic conditions in the United States: the incarcerated.[15] The United States today incarcerates more human beings than any other nation. Its prison sentences are harsher than any other democracy. A minor drug offense, something than wouldn't even involve prison in many places, can land someone in prison for decades or even for life. But the stigma and punishment of prison does not end upon one's release. Convicted felons are legally discriminated against in employment, housing, education and voting rights.

Why is it that the United States deals so harshly with crime? To understand that, one must let go of the notion that "crime" has anything to do with mass incarceration. Harsher sentences came out of the "law and order" politics of the post-civil rights era. As the overt racism of Jim Crow became illegal and socially unacceptable, a new political discourse came into being in which coded language was used to create laws that clearly discriminated against African Americans. Far more African Americans are in prison in spite of the fact that they make up a much smaller proportion of the population and, astonishingly, commit no more crimes, proportionally, than whites. So the liberal notion that so many African Americans are imprisoned is due to poverty which leads to crime actually must be turned upside down: The evidence actually suggests that mass incarceration causes poverty, and that the incarcerated represent a social caste.

The consequences for the African American community have been devastating. Imagine living in a community in which a third or more of the adult males are either incarcerated or denied their basic civil rights because of being labeled a felon. Mass incarceration not only destroys individuals; it also destroys the families and communities of the incarcerated. Moreover, the political climate of the United States as a whole has been affected by mass incarceration. While felons—mostly black or brown people who would vote Democratic—are denied the right to vote, prisoners—mostly in rural, Republican leaning districts—are counted in the populations of the districts in which their prisons are located.[16] But if this weren't enough to skew the electorate in a more conservative direction, mass incarceration has been part of the broader political effort to use "criminals" to elicit fear of black and brown people amongst the populace. Instead of identifying with their economic class and voting for policies that would benefit the poor and working classes, poor whites routinely vote against their self-interests due to a political climate of fear of *the other*.

Incarceration on this scale can be shown to be linked clearly with the American systems of slavery and Jim Crow. While we don't use the language of race, there is no doubt as to who the intended victims of this system are. As with Jim Crow and slavery, the real purpose for putting so many people behind bars has nothing to do with safety (indeed, "safety" was also given as a reason for Jim Crow). Rather, mass incarceration is a means to allow for the maintenance of an inequitable economic system.

In terms of economics, there can be no more marginalized group than the incarcerated. The question must be asked: how sustainable is a civilization that incarcerates so many of its people? Another way to ask the question is this: How close to the end is such a civilization? It must not be forgotten that Jesus was executed as a prisoner of the state. In his time, he and the many impoverished Jews forced into slavery would be the equivalent of today's incarcerated. Deprived of their freedom due to their economic and ethnic status, such people have reached the economic edge from which there is nowhere to turn but to completely re-imagine, as Jesus did, our world.

* * * * *

The second group is, in some senses, the opposite of the imprisoned. Rather than being deprived of the right to move freely, this group is forced, due to economic conditions, to move. These are the migrants, those who have left their home place to find work.

There is, I would suggest, a general misunderstanding about why people leave their home places to find work elsewhere.[17] Much of the discourse in wealthy countries has to do with the greatness of the countries to which people are seeking to come and the gratefulness they should feel toward those wealthy nations for having been permitted to leave their own inferior country. But the process by which a person becomes a migrant has nothing to with where one wants to live. It is surely the case that most migrants would rather remain in their home places. But they are forced to move for the survival of their families due to economic circumstances beyond their control.

While it is undeniable that migrant workers are not a new phenomenon, it is equally true that globalization has led to their proliferation. One of the things globalization does is eliminate space and place as an economic factor. Goods are moved throughout the globe as though this movement has no cost, or at most a nominal one. The real cost of this movement, of course, is manifold. First and foremost, there is an ecological cost of the movement of goods that is not sufficiently accounted for in most economic models. But there is also a human cost: human beings are forced to move in order to find work. There is no longer value in the traditional relationship between work and place. Whereas the traditional economy allowed for a locally embedded and diversified farm to prosper and the traditional craftsman to thrive, the new economy prefers the efficiency of the factory model, be it a farm or a sweatshop. Gandhi's economic theory advocated a return to the traditional craftsman and recognized his marginalization as a part of colonialism. Globalization is an extension of this. And because of the new economic reality, laborers often can no longer thrive in their home places. They are forced to move.

In North America, for example, NAFTA has created economic conditions in which Mexican farmers can no longer support themselves. When government subsidized corn is shipped from the United States, Mexican farmers are forced to look for work. They often end up in the United States. In fact, American firms actively recruit illegal Mexican workers, knowing they will be cheaper. Entire sectors of the economy are based on cheap, illegal labor.

This movement comes in several steps. First, the rural people in poor countries often flock to big cities. They can be found in the shantytowns that surround these emerging megalopolises. Next, the poor often migrate to wealthier countries. The tensions on the US-Mexican border and in the Mediterranean reflect this massive movement. And while many Europeans and Americans act as though they are under siege, most migrants would surely prefer the opportunity to feed their families in their home places. But they often cannot because their traditional economies have been undermined by globalization.

And the life of the migrant is a hard one. Perhaps most difficult is the life of those who come to the oil-producing Gulf States, where factors including an economy based on oil and a small local population have led thousands of South Asian and Filipino migrants to perform the menial tasks that locals will not do. As in Europe and North America, oil leads to imbalance. The abuse of these migrants is widespread. So we can see here the interconnection between an unsustainable civilization, economic inequality and moral decay.

The parallels to the conditions of the people Jesus spoke to in his day are striking. Jesus was clearly a member of a group that had lost its capacity to continue to sustain itself without movement. His activism was born of this movement. He told stories to men and women who had come to urban areas to look for work, men and women at the margins, backs against the wall. Like the incarcerated, migrants are forced into impossible choices. They have reached the edge. This was the context for Jesus' re-imagining of his world, of his new stories. Perhaps it is more likely that such a new story will arise today on the edges of one of our cities than in the centers of its power.

* * * * *

The last group is found at every level of every society, and consequently has perhaps the greatest potential to undermine global Capitalism. These are the indebted. During the Occupy Wall Street Movement, the indebtedness of the youth was a major issue. Increasingly, young people are pressured into taking out costly loans for an education of which the value is uncertain. Feeling trapped upon graduation by these burdensome loans, the youth no longer have the freedom to explore their world, to travel, to create something meaningful, to take risks.

Other members of society are faring no better. Consumer debt has never been higher;[18] skyrocketing medical costs are leaving the sick particularly vulnerable to indebtedness. Farmers, pressured or forced to buy the newest seeds and the latest technology, are trapped by big agribusiness in cycles of debt. They no longer feel that they have the freedom to grow diverse and locally-based crops.

Nations suffer just as individuals do. The indebtedness of African countries, often due to policies of the Global North through such agencies as the IMF, has been well documented. It remains a key factor in keeping Africa poor and under the thumb of their former colonial oppressors.

But this is not a new phenomenon. In Jesus' time, indebtedness was one of the great issues facing his people. Already at the margins of society, indebtedness could push a family over the brink. They could become enslaved or destitute. Indeed, the mass incarceration referred to above cannot be separated from the indebted. An indebted person is truly one with her back against the wall. Jesus confronts this in Matthew's version of The Lord's Prayer: "Forgive us our debts, as we forgive our debtors."[19]

Jesus seemed to have perceived that debt was also a spiritual crisis. That is to say, debt is something of the human imagination. First, while many have no choice but to go into debt, there are also others, particularly in wealthy countries, who feel pressure to do so. Increasingly identifying ourselves as consumers above all else, we buy things we cannot afford and don't need. Moreover, indebtedness is an abstraction. African countries, like those individuals who owe money to insurance companies or banks, could easily be "forgiven". This word—forgiven—is significant. It implies that the indebted have done something wrong, something sinful—an odd attitude for a civilization supposedly based upon a religion founded by a man who said, "Blessed are the poor."[20] It speaks to the religious nature of Capitalism, equating poverty with sinfulness and wealth with salvation.

* * * * *

In general, we have created an economy based on abstraction.[21] That is to say, money, which once was used merely as a way to ascribe value to things, has become an end in itself. As mentioned above, space is no longer an issue in our economy. Goods are moved without regard to the ecological cost. In fact, things themselves are no longer primary. Money is. The 2008 financial crisis, in which increasingly abstract units of mortgages were sold throughout the world's economy, infecting the entire planet with certain bad or "subprime" mortgages, demonstrates the dangers of an increasingly abstract economy.

But there is a deeper, and more apocalyptic, danger in the abstract economy, in a civilization based no longer on things we can touch and feel. Just as the Protestant Reformation and the broader movement of Modernity led us to find meaning in the abstract, the Modern economy has led us to find *value* in the abstract. Some abstraction, of course, can be helpful. It can help to spread prosperity. It can bring goods to places that otherwise wouldn't have them. It can bring help to make ideas applicable in different contexts. But context is important, and completely losing touch with it can deprive us of some of that which makes life so rich.

The economic crisis today, as in Jesus' time, is revelatory in the sense that it pushes people to the edge. Through those at the edge, the disinherited, a deeper truth about our world is revealed. Jesus understood that a new world was only possible with the creative energy of those pushed to this edge.

*   *   *   *   *

So we stand here at the edge of an idea, of a Capitalism that has become so ideological that it approaches a religion in its dogmatism, a dogmatism that threatens to destroy the very flexibility and openness that makes it possible. Freedom has become an idea that enslaves, that obfuscates a clear understanding of our economic condition. Its priests protect against all heresies with a means of control far more powerful than any inquisition: the idea that our system is natural and rational. Beliefs most deeply held come to us in the mysterious form of what we tend to call reality.

The Italian Marxist theorist and activist Franco "Bifo" Berardi suggests that the root of this skewed view of the economy is found in language.[22] A system of abstract finance is expressed in a similarly abstract language. It is the language of the disembodied, the machine. The way forward, according to Berardi, is to return to the poetic. That is to say that the Citizens United decision and the Right Wing order it supports cannot be addressed merely by pleas to a more rational approach—although it would be more rational to, say, create an economy that accounted for the real, ecological cost of things—because the theological assumptions we have made conflate that order with Reason itself.

One challenge we face is that, as was the case for Martin Luther (with the printing press), the information revolution of our day (the Internet) leads us to a more disembodied life. Perhaps we do not need 95 theses nailed to doors of the Supreme Court—much less to blog about it—but stand at its doors and cry out with our embodied, poetic voice.

* * * * *

WHAT WOULD A NEW ECONOMY LOOK LIKE? It is difficult to see beyond Capitalism because it is so woven into our worldview. Lifting the veil requires something like an apocalypse, an imaginative effort far more complex than merely changing a few government policies. It is an opposition Capitalism that lies at the root of many fundamentalist movements. (Indeed, it should be noted that Capitalism does far more harm on the planet today than terrorism). But fundamentalism represents a failure of the imagination—and speaks to the challenge of this imaginative effort in the stifling conditions of consumerism. Indeed, there is nothing wrong with markets per se. Rather, our challenge is to create economies that recognize ecology as primary and that see life—including the non-human, including vibrant and diverse cultural activity, and including a rich interior life—as more important than consumption.

An economy is an expression of values. And values and spirituality go hand in hand. Our spiritual lives—that is, how we understand our place in the cosmos—give rise to our systems, including the economy. Capitalism and Calvinism go hand in hand. When we believe that we are fundamentally individuals, in competition with one another, and that we are not connected to the Earth but ultimately separate from it, we will have an economic system that reflects that.

I've noticed that most people are at least as unsure as I am about what a new economy might look like. This shows how deeply immersed in Capitalism we are. It's actually pretty hard to imagine another system. Marx tried, and the Soviet model showed how difficult it really can be to implement another model. In order to avoid some of these mistakes, we would be well served by starting with a deep examination of the values of a re-imagined spirituality rather than start with a new economic model. The hope would be that out of these values, a viable alternative can emerge organically.

The spiritual principle of equality is an easy place to start because most of us have some intuitive sense that at least humans are all of equal value. But this can be tricky in practice. To what extent do we work to create an egalitarian society? Again, for most of human history, people lived in what, by today's standards, were radically egalitarian communities. But the advent of Capitalism—the ability to save and inherit wealth that increases with time—has led to an increasingly inegalitarian planet. While it is true that there have been periods of greater equality (post-World War II, for example), this is largely due to the fact that the economy was growing rapidly, which is largely due to the ability to increase populations and exploit new markets. We are approaching an age of low or, perhaps, zero growth, and this will lead to greater inequality. In fact, it is already is happening.[23]

There is a specific, if partial, remedy to this problem within the parameters of the current system. A global tax on capital[24] could be implemented, which would provide money to alleviate poverty and to allow for investment in alternative energies. It would, moreover, reduce the absurd overconsumption of the wealthy. Such an action, while admittedly politically difficult on a global scale, must be global because (a) climate change is global and (b) the current economy is globalized; money moves freely.

For this value to truly take root would require more, however, than a vague sense of equality. At its core, the radical opposition of such prophets as Jesus (to be explored further in chapter 8) to inequality must be fully understood and embraced as a spiritual principle. A global tax on capital must be implemented because inequality leads, ultimately, to the capacity of one person to buy another and the compulsion of another to sell herself. Whether we call this a "free market" or slavery is mere semantics; it is the inevitable result of an inegalitarian system.

Second is the spirituality of meaningful, embodied work. Each of us should be able to find both meaning in our work and engage our bodies in the process of production. Sitting in cubicles, moving money around to make more money for the rich not only exacerbates inequality; it also moves us further and further from real and meaningful work. It drives us deeper into abstraction and alienation from the natural world.

Third is the spirituality of enough. On an individual level, many of the great traditions embrace the notion that true fulfillment is found not in always looking for more, but in recognizing that we already have enough. But what would this look like on a collective, global scale? It is profoundly important to examine this question as we approach the end of Capitalism, for the simple fact of the end of Capitalism is that we can no longer have a growing economy on a finite planet stretched to its very limit. The apocalyptic nature of this moment lies largely in this fact—that the cosmology of consumption is ending.

This challenges the core values of our economy. For example, the concept of the GDP is used by politicians of all political persuasions to indicate the health of an economy. Of course, this indicator does not account for externalities: growth is always good, even if we destroy our forests and seas in the process, even if it incarcerates millions and starts wars. Alternatively, a zero-growth economy would account for the true cost of things. The profits of an oil company that destroys the planet would not be viewed as profits at all, because their true costs far outweigh their benefits.

Lastly, the spirituality of interconnection is a way to value all beings. The essential problem with our economy is that we value things—from humans to forests—in terms of money rather than in their intrinsic value as beings. The forests are not valuable because they produce wood, or even because they are a nice place for people to go camping. They have value just like you and me, because we exist and have the right to be.

* * * * *

There is always an alternative. But when a system is so deeply embedded in the psyche, a profound act of the imagination is required. And until we challenge the values behind Capitalism, there will indeed appear to be no alternative. Of course, total collapse will bring about a change as well. Whether Capitalism ends through a re-imagining or a collapse, or both, it has reached its apocalyptic moment.

Chapter 5

The Farming Revolution and the New Spirituality

JUST AS WE ARE ALL NATURE, we are all, essentially, farmers. Very few of us would survive for very long without farms. Our lives and, indeed, civilization itself, are completely dependent upon the existence of farms. But one of the deep paradoxes of Modernity is that, at the same time, none of us is a farmer, either—or at least very few of us. We are completely alienated from the one process that we all depend on more than any other, the growing of food.

Because it is so integral to human culture, we cannot entirely separate our consciousness from farming. For example, methods we use in farming today influence and are influenced by our culture. Specifically, I would suggest that one cannot have a factory farm system without also having a factory *school* system. They co-create one another; they co-arise. In the past, as we shall see, the way that human beings farmed and fed themselves was integrated inextricably with human culture and spirituality.

What cannot be avoided, however, is the apocalyptic nature of industrial agriculture. It has, for all its productivity, led us to the very edge of planetary capacity—to such a degree that a crash seems imminent. There is no way forward without a radical change in farming methods, which cannot happen without a re-imagined spirituality.

* * * * *

I once lived on a Zimbabwean dairy farm. I had no particular connection to or expertise in farming. Rather, I was housed there while I worked for an NGO in an adult literacy program. I heard the lowing cows each morning as they were milked, listened to their cries as their calves were weaned. But my work was beyond the farm, in a rural area that was entirely made up of subsistence farms. Each day, I would walk to our lessons through the parched countryside, through the dry and overworked and depleted soils, cracking under our feet. These were the lands where the poor Zimbabweans were forced to live and sustain themselves, while the white farmers had come to claim the good lands for their commercial farms.

Zimbabwe was in a state of upheaval when I arrived. The currency had collapsed. In the years that followed, groups of armed men would begin to take over the wealthy white farms. This happened with the ruling government's full support; but it was not because those in power were interested in justice for the rural poor. It happened because Zimbabwe was on the edge. The rural areas were overcrowded; the soils dry and pushed to their limit; deforestation, in a land in which wood was the primary fuel, was rampant. Urban shantytowns were overflowing with migrants.

Land and the growing of food are always central to the unfolding of apocalypse. While in Zimbabwe, as in any other example, there were many factors—the global economy, the legacy of colonialism, the injustice of land distribution, the incompetence and brutality of the Mugabe regime—when a people loses the ability to sustain itself on the land, unraveling follows. Apocalypse follows. It has seldom been mentioned that Syria's civil war, among the most brutal in recent memory, is partly rooted in a drought linked to climate change.

Communities unravel and cultures disintegrate when the land no longer produces food. There is no faster road to apocalypse. We like to think that we are different, those of us who live in wealthy, peaceful places, for whom wars are fought thousands of miles away with drones. We do not get involved in the messy, dirty, bloody business of war in the way that we hear about on the television—genocides and ethnic cleansing, mass rape and mass execution. But the truth is that we are only a few failed crops away from such brutality. The truth is that we fool our selves into thinking we are any different from the people who commit atrocities. Of course, many would not—just as many resisted the Nazis and the *interahamwe*—but many, too many, would descend into madness when they fear they cannot feed their children.

In the coming years, water will be central in many of our wars. Climate change and the depletion of soils due to industrial agriculture will lead to crisis after crisis, conflict after conflict. There will be two options: the shock doctrine of crisis Capitalism—using crisis to benefit the few at the expense of the poor masses, which is essentially a more extreme application of the current worldview—or the great re-imagining. A new way of farming and of life.

* * * * *

The agricultural revolution is often portrayed as an invention of a group of clever people. But it would be more accurate to think of agriculture as evolving in the context of human ecological relationships. The primordial human culture was one of embeddedness in nature and interrelatedness. The corresponding spirituality was one of *enchantment*. The cosmos—defined by the ecological community—was alive and sacred. Human identity was inextricable from this web. The relationship between humans and our sources of food was a sacred one—and in a world in which none of the false guarantees of the supermarket exist, there would have been nothing more central or important than this relationship. In time, slowly, the relationship between human settlement and food would have given rise to evolutionary changes: animals that once were followed or chased by humans began to live among them; the seeds that grew from human waste were now planted intentionally. All this is evolution; it is relationship. There is no absolute dualism as in industrial farming.

An increasingly settled relationship and a more intentional relationship between humans and food gave rise to an evolution in spirituality. The farmer began to see the world in terms of the balance between mother and father gods, the Earth's fertility being paramount. At the same time, the pastoralist, still a nomad, developed a more patriarchal form of spirituality. God, already gendered, became exclusively male. These two forms of spirituality remained embedded in the axial religions that would later become our primary world religions. The monotheists would look to the sky for their father god; the Taoists, for example, would add layers of philosophical complexity and interiorization to the dialectic of mother and father gods. In Hinduism these elements were integrated—the Aryans bringing with them their father god in the Vedas, but the indigenous Great Mother remaining part of the complex and pluralistic world that gave rise, in the axial age, to Vedanta.

The axial religions arose in the context of Empire—complex, hierarchical, pluralistic, and militarized civilizations. The old gods were first coopted for the purposes of empire: the sacred mountain or tree was moved to the temple of the emperor. It must be understood that such a civilization could only exist with large-scale agriculture, which allows for a military class and other elites. And the structure of such civilizations dictates the structure of consciousness.

It is in the context of empire that apocalypse first appears. Empire—deeply related to today's global Capitalism—devoirs all in its path. The peacemakers can do little to stop what is commonly referred to as its "progress". For militarism simply leads to their destruction. And those who win the wars and expand empires do so not due to their bravery in battle, but because they had the resources—the agricultural production—to produce the demographic advantage of a military class. Empire is irresistible. The only escape was apocalypse, and the interior transformations that the axial religions provided.

* * * * *

Farming remained, however, central to human culture for millennia. Those who were able to remove themselves from the process of food production had always, even after the agricultural revolution and the advent of imperial societies, been the minority. Most people were farmers, and pre-Modern religion, even the more dualistic and patriarchal versions, remained rooted in agricultural metaphors and symbolism.

This began to change, however, as the Modern era ushered in a separation of science—the physical world and Nature—from religion—the internal, immaterial, psychic world. The Protestant Reformation represented the first completely Modern religious movement, in that religion became a personal, interior endeavor, rather than a cosmic and communal one. A rejection of matter and of the physical body was part and parcel of this movement. People were still farmers, but farming was not, for the Protestant, a labor of love. It was an act of conquest. Colonialism expanded rapidly as it was now seen as God's work, taming the wild and the wilderness—making it holy by making it more human, more sterile, more cultivated.

The patterns of alienation from the land begun through Capitalism, colonialism, and Protestantism were completed with industrial revolution. This impacted the culture and consciousness of farming in two ways. First, it brought people increasingly into cities in which they sold their labor to work in factories rather than grow their food. Second, it brought about an industrialization of the farm itself.

The transformation that has occurred in farming during the last fifty years arises directly out of the industrial revolution. The link between farming and ecology, the creativity of the individual farmer and the local nature and subsequent diversity of the farm have all been lost. Industrial Capitalism, applied to the farm, has alienated farmer and eco-system, and the effects have been devastating. No longer a means for fostering relationship, the farm has become, like industrial civilization as a whole, a destructive force on the planet. Chemical fertilizer that had been developed during the world wars for weaponry has been applied in such a way that soils are depleted and pollution from farming is nearly as bad as from factories.[25] And while initially leading to a huge increase in outputs—the so-called "green revolution"—factory farms are putting our ability to feed our selves increasingly at risk as soils are depleted and water sources are toxified.

The farm, once a place where humans danced at the edge of civilization and the wild, a controlled but diverse ecology, has become sterile. It now limits genetic and biological diversity rather than preserving it as it once did. A trip to farm country in the United States is to encounter mile after mile of corn and soy, corn and soy, as far as the eye can see. The reasons for this have nothing to do with efficiency, as agribusiness would claim.

Nor is it the case that human beings would rather eat corn and soy. Politics, and the influence of agribusiness, has led the farmer to this place. Linked to the corn and soy farm is the factory farm, something that looks and operates nothing like what most of us envision when we think of a farm. Animals contained in filthy, disease-ridden spaces, with no room to roam, with diets largely derived from the heavily-subsidized grains of monoculture—you guessed it, soy and corn.

Our entire food production and consumption process has become mechanized, toxified, and perhaps most significantly, desacralized. Indigenous peoples have always understood the sacred act of growing food and sharing a meal. In the rituals of the world's religions, sharing a meal is a recurrent theme. In Christianity, the Communion celebration is a core ritual—but how sacred is the body of Christ when the bread is grown without the loving care of the farmer?

* * * * *

There is, however, another kind of revolution happening on the planet today, akin to the great upheavals of the agricultural and industrial revolutions. It is largely unnamed and, because so few of us are in any way involved in farming or food production, largely unnoticed. It is a movement that involves a variety of organic and holistic farming practices, including the permaculture and bio-dynamic farming movements. Collectively, I will refer to them as Agro-Ecology, because I believe that the key philosophical shift that must occur is to see farming as an integral part of ecology rather than an industrial process.

Understanding the relational evolutionary nature of ecology is essential in order to create sustainable farming practices. We have based our current farming on the industrial worldview. That worldview—and, indeed, the world it feeds—is falling apart. Soils are depleted; pollution from farms is worse than most cities. Soon, the massive production made possible by fossil fuels will crash. A deep ecological sensibility requires that the human not only understand ecology as it relates to other organisms, but also recognize—and not just recognize, but actually *feel*—that the human is another organism in this web.

There is a return to smaller scales implicit in these new practices. Although they could still happen, theoretically, on large scales, farming on small scales requires more people to be involved in the process. It requires less alienation from the process and makes accessible the wealth of enriching activities that come from producing food.

In permaculture, the basic model for a garden is a series of "zones" laid out in a pattern of concentric circles. This is an ecological model. It is also the model for a mandala. The human is at the center; wildness lies at the edges. But when we see ourselves as mandalas, we recognize that we are the whole mandala; the whole mandala is us. We are the whole ecosystem; the whole ecosystem is us.

And just as the farm itself can only be understood as an interconnected whole through space—no separation between humans, beans and corn, animals—the process of food production is a single thread—a sutra, to borrow a term from the East—connected temporally from seed to table. When we grow our food and process our food and prepare our food, we become healthier spiritually and physically. "There is, then, a politics of food that, like any politics, involves our freedom," writes Wendell Berry. "We still (sometimes) remember that we cannot be free if our minds and voices are controlled by someone else. But we have neglected to understand that we cannot be free if our food and its sources are controlled by someone else… One reason to eat responsibly is to live free."[26] Eating is political and spiritual. All the *information* about new diets and healthy lifestyles seem to go hand and hand with an increasingly unhealthy population. We know more about health and diet, but eat less healthy. The so-called "first world diseases" of heart disease, diabetes, and cancer ravish the United States, the home of "health food". The problem lies not with our nutritional knowledge but in the decoupling of food and culture, and culture is rooted in ecology. We shouldn't think about what we eat; we should work the land, grow healthy food and share it.

* * * * *

The Agro-ecology revolution will change human consciousness just as the Agricultural Revolution and the Industrial Revolution did. It will re-introduce us to the sacredness of nature and the wild. Moreover, human communities—Earth communities—will emerge as part of ecological community. Indeed, the notion of spirituality as an individual pursuit rather than a communal one is undermined by the recognition that the food we eat is community, too.

These are apocalyptic changes. Today's worldview is completely shaped by the factory farm and its alienations. Its loneliness. Its brutality. We consume it every day. It is in our bodies. Indeed, it is in our souls.

Chapter 6

The Tech Revolution
Mindfulness in an Age of Distraction

When was the last time you were alone? I mean really alone—not connected to the global monoculture through a smart phone or wifi. It is likely that it's been a while, or at least that such moments have been infrequent. For most of us, something has happened very recently that has transformed our consciousness and literally reshaped the human brain. We will call it the Tech Revolution. We have entered the information age.

It is telling that the focus in this age is on *information.* It is not, as those who would suggest that human progress is always a straight line of improvement would expect, the age of wisdom. We seem no better equipped to process the information we have, no more capable of using information to live more meaningful and compassionate lives. In keeping with the ethos of consumerism, it is simply *more*. The values of the information age—Facebook and Google its chief evangelists—dictate that sharing more information is always better and that increased connectivity is always better.

* * * * *

Before I explore the Tech Revolution more broadly, a personal perspective. It fills me with sadness to see faces lightened by phones rather than lighting up the world with their presence. It is particularly sad to see this in the youth, who never have had a chance. They do not remember an unconnected time. Most have never had the experience of being alone. They sleep with televisions buzzing, phones under their pillows. They look at me, mystified, a forty-two-year old who chooses to live without a smart phone. But still, I am rarely disconnected. March from email to email, text to text. While my screen-time might be far less than most, I still feel the addicting pull of social media and the Internet in general, luring me away from the world, from my self, from community, with the seduction of information and facile connectivity.

I traveled a lot in the nineties. We were truly in the beginnings of the tech revolution then, but it had not yet taken full flight. Although it wasn't long ago, it is astonishing how much has changed since then. No one had cell phones. Many didn't use the Internet or have email. We couldn't see the changes on the horizon. And it was possible, still, to find one's way to a place where one could be truly alone, even if few people ever did.

But I did. I traveled to Africa, to beaches without tourists in South America, to wild deserts in the Middle East and to China before it really opened up. I found my way by talking to people, by trusting that the bus would take me to the right place, even without GPS. And although I found Internet cafes in many places, I lay down each night alone, contemplating the stars or the adventures I'd had. True adventure, like the stars for urban people, is almost gone. Lostness is almost gone.

* * * * *

To understand the impact of the tech revolution it would be useful to find a historical corollary. Literacy is perhaps the only cultural phenomenon that compares. Plato reported that Socrates warned against the dangers of the written word as opposed to the spoken.[27] For indigenous peoples, the writing down of sacred stories is often considered dangerous, for it concretizes the words. Stories lose their flexibility. The fundamental process of human language—the fluid and dynamic engagement of speaker and listener in a process—is lost. In Greek terms, this led to a movement away from poetic or mythic thinking and communicating to the logical—from *mythos* to *logos.*

Writing and reading requires abstract thinking. Good writing, however, allows us to enter into another world that involves the whole person. It is a mental act, an abstraction, which calls attention to embodied connections we have. And, of course, reading and writing has always happened with a book in the hand. Pages turned. Moreover, as a mental act of following a story, a narrative, or an argument from beginning to end, it allows for a level of attention that quiets the mind from all its myriad distractions.

Writing truly began to shift human consciousness with the invention of the printing press. It is no mere coincidence that this invention was contemporaneous with the Protestant Reformation. For all its benefits—and there are many—the printing press made it possible for a truly Modern religious movement to emerge in Europe. It was a movement based on the absolute isolation of the individual. Separate from Nature, from community, from the body, spirituality was reduced to a psychological process, a process that was mediated primarily through reading the Bible.

This could be viewed as the first revolution in the Information Age. It shaped consciousness in such a way that it emphasized the abstract over the embodied, and the linear logic of the written narrative over the symbolic and mythic meaning of the pre-Modern era. What is important to emphasize is that it did not, in spite of the abstract character of reading and writing, move us away from many of the traditional narratives as the basic way that the human makes meaning. Nor did it move us away from mindfulness. The printing press, in its emphasis on the written word, brought with it benefits and problems, like all new technologies. While it did, in fact, move us away from a more embodied and less abstract form of consciousness, it also emphasized a particular type of mindfulness and opened it up to the masses. Now, anyone with access to a library could discover the world through a book. And they could do so with the focused, mindful attention that reading requires. While many have lauded the Internet as providing similar access to the masses, it also brings with it a new challenge, particularly as it relates to mindfulness.

* * * * *

The character of the Tech Revolution is such that it favors radical individualism. Each new technology not so much gives us greater access to greater things; rather, it allows us to experience those things individually. For instance, the VCR didn't mean we had better movies, it merely meant we could watch the same movies alone. The Internet has increased this individual experience, and the smart phone has intensified this further.

This is worth unpacking a bit. First, it is impossible to miss that this radical individualism is connected to consumer Capitalism. The Internet focuses on shopping and an enhanced, individualized form of advertising—to the point that, through social media, content and advertisement are difficult to separate. Second, individualized technologies have largely been produced because of the desire for pornography. Before VCRs, there wasn't much demand to watch movies at home; but there was a demand, for obvious reasons, to watch pornography at home. The Internet's growth has been similarly driven by the porn industry. These two interrelated concepts—pornography and consumerism—have come to dominate our mental space and our culture.

* * * * *

The Internet, just as it allows for the dissemination and processing of information to expand exponentially, also brings about shifts in human consciousness exponentially. To understand this transformation, one must recognize the plasticity of the human brain. Something more is happening than changed habits.

The Internet is arranged in such a way that it de-emphasizes thoughtful, focused attention. The screen, by its very design, encourages us to click and move. And the brain, shaped now at an early age by new technologies, begins to expect them. Social media is actually designed to create an addiction to such a lack of focus. Our brains have a chemical response when someone likes a Facebook post or follows us on Twitter. We feel good. We look for more. Of course, all these are two-dimensional, shallow responses. While the chemical reaction might not be so different from sharing food with a friend or a hug from a loved one, they are ephemeral by nature; there is no lasting connection, only the yearning for more. The Capitalist ethos of more is experienced now, socially.

All this is intensified by the technologies that give us immediate access to these platforms. The smartphone has become, for many, an extension of the human body. We feel we cannot live without it. We are connected every minute of every day, seeking, like the addict, another hit.

What has been lost in this process is that we seem to have become more machine than human. The depth, the three-dimensional, textured experiences that make up a good life, which make us human, are lost. This loss has altered the human brain and is radically transforming human culture. There are many—perhaps most—who would describe this transformation as good. And there are indeed good things about it—access to information is a benefit, for example. But there are also many problems.

First, technology is something of a false prophet, a promise of a quick fix that never comes. And, in fact, it distracts us from the real, more difficult solutions. Recall the assessment of technology as the solution to climate change. Without a change in attitude about consumption—*metanoia*—new technologies alone lead only to more consumption.

Moreover, access to more information does not give one the ability to discern what is useful or correct information, nor does it give one the wisdom to use the information sensibly. Human beings process information holistically, and we are experiencing the world less holistically with greater reliance on these technologies. Human beings process information through narratives (more on that in chapter 10), which require imagination, not merely information.

The addictive nature of our gadgets and of the Internet, particularly social media, leads to a profound loss of mindfulness. We are constantly connected and, oddly, disconnected. That is, we have lost the constant attention and presence in our cultural, communal and ecological context that gives us our sense of place in and peace with the world. We end up, like the addict, on edge, looking for the next hit, never satisfied with what lies in front of us.

It is worth making a distinction at this point between community and network. While the word community is thrown around rather carelessly ("on-line community") it is actually more accurate to describe the mediated spaces of the Internet as networks. That is, it is designed to direct us to those who will reflect back to us our own viewpoints. Moreover, the kinds of connections made through these networks remain two-dimensional. We only know the surface positions of people, not their deep, holistic selves. We are capable, in community, of finding common ground with people with whom we disagree because we learn to know them in a deeper, more nuanced way. Such knowledge is only possible in the context of a whole community—spaces in which we are touching one another, communicating non-verbally, and building lasting relationships. None of this happens in the on-line network.

Of course, there is also an appeal to the network that pulls us away from community. Networks re-affirm our beliefs and values rather than challenge them. They allow us to present ourselves as we wish, for we have greater control over what comes through in the network. Networks, to put it simply, are less messy and challenge us less than communities.

* * * * *

It is this movement away from the three-dimensional, textured life that must be challenged. The Buddhist concept of mindfulness—although one need not be Buddhist to be mindful—best describes the spiritual practice of living one's life in three dimensions. It is a question, perhaps, of tasting the world, a metaphor used by many of the world's mystical traditions about true religious experience. The question, for us all, is the extent to which we actually are tasting even our own lives. Do we feel our bodies, the elements outside? Are we attentive to our personal relationships?

Much effort has been put forth in the Modern world to sterilize. We no longer want to feel, because feeling—much like the wildness explored in chapter 2—is scary. It requires us to be emotionally vulnerable. A screen is safe. A car is safe. We risk much less living behind metal and glass or in front of a screen. Of course, we are all slowly dying in our cars and in front of our screens. We are losing so much of what makes us human.

* * * * *

There is a sense that I suspect most people have that there is a freedom to be found on-line, or through the smart phone. It is ironic, however, that it is the addictive quality of these things that tethers us to them. They have become chains, like the gold chains of Capitalism for the shopping addict. The line between human and machine has become so blurred that one has to ask: who is in charge, the human being or the phone? Who is making the decisions?

There is a totalitarianism in the tech revolution perhaps more comprehensive than any Orwellian government. By totalitarianism, I refer to the completeness of control over mind, body and spirit that these technologies—and the few corporations that control and mediate these technologies—now hold. Control is enacted by the demonization of privacy. Everything is shared. Indeed, we begin, in subtle but undeniable ways, to deny the reality of that which is not shared and stored and recorded in the information cloud. Later, in chapter 12, we will explore how the privileging of disembodied information is a form of Manichean dualism that represents the ultimate end, or apocalypse, of the Information Age, and of the dualistic streak in Western philosophy, stretching back to the Hellenistic Age.

At play here again is the close relationship between false freedom and loneliness. To be free of deep, human relationships—and this is the kind of freedom the

Information Age promises—is the ultimate loneliness. It would be useful to introduce another term for the sake of distinction: solitude. For solitude and loneliness, while they both are found in being alone, are opposites of human experience. Solitude is the healthy space in which to practice mindfulness. In various traditions, from East to West, solitude is an important spiritual practice. In the Christian tradition, for example, the desert fathers initiated the monastic tradition as a response to the ways in which Christianity was being coopted and watered down by Roman society. It was no longer countercultural, but a part of mainstream society. The desert fathers did not believe that true Christianity could occur in this context—for they took seriously the apocalyptic teachings of Christ; they understood that Jesus had called for a complete transformation of the soul and society, that Jesus did not believe salvation and empire could be reconciled without an apocalypse. In their solitude, the desert fathers found not only a benefit from the absence of conventional society, but also from the presence of the mindful practices that were only possible in solitude.

For Buddhists, solitude and mindfulness is primary. Buddhism begins not with ideas but with practices intended to awaken the individual to reality—eventually revealing the illusory nature of absolute individualism. Awakening requires mindful practices. In a way, Buddhism provides a template for facing the ultimate illusion of the tech revolution. For the illusion of the world of the Internet is only an extension of the human tendency to delude oneself with attachments and addictions. The Buddha saw this thousands of years before the advent of the computer.

* * * * *

It could be said, therefore, that the Tech Revolution is the ultimate end—the apocalypse—of what I will call techno-abstraction. It promises freedom, but in reality only provides loneliness; it promises connection, but provides only networks devoid of community; it promises knowledge, but provides only information without meaning. In a broader context, we may understand the Tech Revolution as the ultimate end of an apocalyptic process of abstraction, not unrelated to the other journeys we have undertaken toward abstraction in economics and ecological relationships.

Perhaps the revelation at this stage is to discover a new monasticism.

Chapter 7

Education at the Edge of the World

CLASSROOM. What is the image that comes to mind? In spite of the time I've spent in alternative educational settings, in spite of the work we've done at The Chicago Wisdom Project[28] to re-imagine education, I still go back to my high school: rows of desks; a teacher standing in the front. There might be a bell that rings at a precise time indicating that it is time to move into the next box.

Much can be said about the ineffectiveness of such a classroom, but I'd like to focus for a moment on the deeper narrative that is being played out in such spaces. For a school's significance is not merely the information it can impart; far more impactful is the way a school creates a metaphor for the world. A school is, in fact, a little world, teaching its students not only a bunch of discrete facts but also way to think about the world.

So what is the image of the world that this classroom projects? First, we are teaching our students that the world is *dualistic*. There are teachers and there are students, bosses and workers, rich and poor, saved and damned. A clear line is drawn between the teacher and the student. Second, it teaches that our world is *hierarchical*. Power resides in the teacher. Our goal is not to empower our selves or one another, but to somehow access the power that lies in the other. Theologically, it speaks to a theistic god, one that is apart from our world. Third, this classroom teaches us that our world is *mechanistic*. Rather than being a wild, creative space, the classroom is one in which control is paramount. The world, therefore, is a machine, too. Fourth, the world of the Modern classroom is based upon *Capitalism*. We are consumers of education, in competition with one another.

* * * * *

Before we can think about an alternative to this system, it would be useful to back up a bit and ask some important questions about education. What does it mean to be an educated human being? During what experiences have you learned the most? These are questions I ask people all time, and the answers are telling. People describe having learned in all different settings: traveling, playing outside, building something, encountering a new place or having a new experience, playing music. Seldom—although it does happen—do people say that their most meaningful learning experience was in a school. People have trouble with the other question. As much as we have opinions about how to improve our schools, seldom have many of us really thought about what makes a person "educated" or successful. (This is interesting: there are a host of opinions about a subject that few people can even actually define). But those who can answer say things like "someone who can think critically" or "someone with curiosity about the world."

Whatever the answers, I then ask people to remove the words "educated" and "learned" from the questions to reframe them as "What does it mean to be a human being?" and "During what experience have you been the most alive?" What is so interesting about this process is that changing the words does not change the answers. To ask someone what it means to be an educated person is to ask what makes her more fully human; to ask a person about moments of deep learning is to ask about moments of being fully alive. The answer to these questions reveals that education is fundamentally a spiritual quest, a journey to become both deeper and more expansive, to become enriched internally and to become more connected to the world beyond our selves.

* * * * *

The Modern model of education provides us with none of these things. This, again, is a spiritual problem, by which I mean it is an educational system based upon the wrong mythology—even the wrong theology.

There are three basic metaphors that we have for education, which are derived from certain core narratives or myths that dominate the Modern world.[29] These metaphors determine everything that happens in the school and the classroom. It would be bad enough if the only problem were the damage done inside the school. But the primary work of a school is to provide a metaphor for the world. A bad metaphor, when employed in a school, re-enforces a bad metaphor for the world.

The first metaphor is the metaphor of the machine. This is based on the cosmology that says our world is a machine. It renders the planet and nature meaningless, good only as a resource to be exploited. It is a useful metaphor if the purpose of schools is to perpetuate an economic system dependent upon the continued exploitation of the planet and unchecked growth. It is also useful in perpetuating the dualism that the spiritual and the material are in opposition.

This dualism, which divides the world into matter and spirit, good and evil, saved and damned, came into Christianity through Greek philosophy and has been a major force in the West throughout history. But it became even more pronounced with the advent of what is known as the Newtonian-Cartesian paradigm, which strictly separated our world into these two categories. Bad theology has a way of transcending even religion. One need not be a practicing Christian to adhere to these notions.

The industrial revolution took this dualism to new heights. As the Universe was conceived of as a vast machine, the world came to be filled with machines. The metaphor became commonplace as more people left agrarian life and moved to cities to work in factories. This was the context of the creation of the public school system as we know it. The students in our high schools were moved along assembly lines like machines or products in order to prepare them for a life working in the factories. As a result, we came to see our world as a machine. This meant both that it was inert, dead, a mere resource to exploit and also that our inner lives were wholly separate from the physical world.

More recently, our schools began to employ the metaphor of the prison. This has been particularly true in poor communities where mass incarceration and racism conspired to criminalize youth. Black and brown children must be treated like criminals in our schools, the logic goes, because they will likely commit crimes when they are older.

Of course, this only deepens the alienation of those young people. Being told they are criminals, unsurprisingly, has the effect of encouraging people to opt out of the system. As Bill Ayers puts it, the drop out rates in our nation's poor urban schools can be seen as a mass protest.[30]

Theologically, there is a deeply Augustinian streak in the school as prison. Our world is a prison from which we must escape. Our communities are prisons from which we must escape. Our world is a prison, not a place to be improved or loved, but merely something from which, in death, we move on to a better place.

Lastly, and most commonly today, is the metaphor of the free market. School districts are now run by "CEOs" rather than superintendents; "Race to the Top" and "No Child Left Behind" employ mass-quantification of the educational process to create a system based on the sterile logic of the free market. We are products, not unlike cell phones or automobiles, valuable in our quantifiable, marketable sameness. And we are also being trained to be consumers—valuable in our capacity to buy.

Moreover, education becomes reducible to its capacity to make the student marketable, competitive in the global economy. The capacity to question the merits of this economic system is never mentioned. And this is, for our purposes here, a most telling omission. For it is the special destructive capacity of this system that has led us to the brink of apocalypse. Indeed, the values of our school system have come to an end.

* * * * *

While it is true that education is important for each individual seeking a better life—a job, for example—there are reasons other than individual ones to focus on education. In other words, as the above examples demonstrate, a school or a classroom's significance is far greater than the individual opportunities it affords. A school, as a metaphor for the world—a microcosm, if you will—gives birth to the world our children will inhabit. The real outcomes of the school are not the tests our children take: they are the narratives that are the soil upon which their lives grow; they are the world we create.

At the edge of the world, at the moment of apocalypse, education becomes perhaps even more significant than ever. For most of human history, we learned as participants in a culture: the songs and stories of our ancestors, the life skills required for survival, the knowledge of cultural norms that allowed for cohesive communities. All education fit, somehow, into humanity's need to find meaning in its basic context, the local ecosystem. Modernity took us away from traditional education, resulting in the educational forms described above. But as our world falls apart—literally and psychically—we must figure out, again, how to live on this planet. We have become a planetary species—there is no going back. So we require a form of education that allows us to live on the planet, just as our ancestors figured out how to live in their forest or on their mountain.

* * * * *

What, then, does education look like in an apocalyptic age? What is most significant about such a moment in human history is that education, rather than providing a core cultural narrative for a small group of people as it did for most of human history, must challenge and re-imagine the narrative. We need a new story, and this can only be done if we have a new way of educating.

So many of our youth have been given what we call a "deficit narrative"—that is, a story that describes them as somehow deficient. If they have not succeeded, they are told, it is due to their own failings rather than the injustices of our society. The work, therefore, is to inspire our youth to tell a new story, a "counter narrative". A new story can only be told with a whole person, and by asking and re-asking the question "Who Am I?" from various perspectives:

Intellectually, our youth must begin to foster critical consciousness, critiquing media, corporate, and political narratives. This is challenging work. Never before in human history have young people spent so much time consuming so much media. Never before have people been privy to so much information with so few skills to actually process it. Much of this narrative is conveyed through advertising, which conflates value with and attributes identity to the products one buys. A re-imagined education, therefore, must give our youth the skills to challenge these narratives. Let me be clear: to succeed in today's educational setting requires one to live a profoundly destructive life. This can only be considered "success" when one thinks of oneself as an isolated individual and a consumer. This is the challenge of deconstructing the myths that have led us to apocalypse.

Emotionally, our youth must do soul work, processing their feelings by creating caring circles, through meditation and through rites of passage. In most educational settings, the emotions are only permitted to enter into the process when there is a problem. A child misbehaves, for example, and is sent to a counselor. But the emotions must be integrated meaningfully into the learning process, woven into the intellectual fabric of education. We learn as much by and through processing our emotions—and allowing space and compassion for others—as from intellectual discourse.

Physically, our youth must learn through embodied practices like martial arts and yoga, as well as building and farming practices. This does not mean that they get a little bit of time to run around while the real, intellectual work is done sitting down; it means that body and mind are integrated, that we learn through doing.

Ecologically, our youth begin to recognize their ecological selves. This is not a question of information about nature, but of identity with nature. Perhaps no other aspect of our education is as neglected as this. For millennia, this would have been central to a young person's education, but we now learn—perhaps not explicitly, but through the various processes in the mechanistic educational system—that we are disconnected, cut off from the natural world. The harm this does to our planet because of the values it conveys is immeasurable. We require not merely to spend time in nature; rather, we must understand that we *are* nature.

After all this—and woven through all this—we return to the story. Through creative expression—any medium, from poetry to pottery, from film to music, can work—our youth can tell their story for themselves. They can become creators of culture, not merely consumers of it. They can become teachers of their peers. And then this process will begin again.

But there is more to re-imagining education than the content. The process is just as important, if not more so. Here is the rub: it can't be a conventional classroom that just talks about different issues—the process and the pedagogy must be re-imagined. Here are some practices that make the re-imagined classroom different:

- Sit in a circle. The teacher is a part of the circle. This is a non-hierarchical space.
- Ask questions. Dialogue is emphasized over lectures, honoring the wisdom of the learner and emphasizing the process over information.
- Learning is embodied, breaking down the patriarchal tendency to separate mind and body and to privilege mind over body.
- Nature is a part—if not all—of the classroom.
- The interior life—emotions and feelings—are a part of every dialogue and should be recognized and honored.

* * * * *

I have often suggested that religion needs to be more educational and that education needs to be more spiritual. What I mean by this is that most of us learn very little in church. I have found, when I teach world religions, that the most difficult groups to teach are the practitioners of the religion we are discussing. There are many reasons for this, but part of it is due to the fact that no one really bothers to teach much about the tradition in most religious communities. Religion is the realm of feeling and community building, not of the intellect.

School, on the other hand is the realm of the intellect or mind. In school, there is no time for the emotional, no time to ask big questions about our place in the world, no time for community because it is only about individual success.

Perhaps what is required is to knock down all the churches and all the schools. Get rid of them altogether. Find learning elsewhere. And perhaps we ought to not build anything in their place. Sit outside in circles. Walk through forests. Tell stories and sing songs. Learn about the traditions of our ancestors and how they answered the Big Questions so that we might find answers of our own. Care for each other. Love each other. This is church. This is school.

* * * * *

The ultimate goal, of course, is not to make a better school or a better church. It is to make more compassionate, just and sustainable communities. This requires an educational process that allows for a re-imagining of the self, recognizing our selves as mandalas, a unique expression of a web of relationships that includes the whole planet, the whole cosmos. We cannot re-discover this without an educational process that facilitates a thorough transformation of human culture. Where, at this apocalyptic moment, might we discover and re-discover this new human? I would suggest that just as we are at the edge of our world right now as a species, there are plenty of places we can look to find people for whom living at the edge is nothing new. We often refer to these people often as "marginalized". And there is a particular wisdom at the margins, for those who reside there have not benefited from the current systems. They see the brokenness of our world. But they also can see the possibilities—if we can create an educational process that allows for them to re-imagine the deficit narratives. The new story, in other words, won't come from the old centers of power. Nor will it emerge if we educate from there.

PART II

BIRTH

Chapter 8

Inversion, Conversion, Subversion

Trickster and Messiah as Revolutionaries

THERE IS A PARTICULAR WISDOM at the margins of our world. As discussed in previous chapters, the narratives and values of a society often seem to be simple logic to those who benefit from them. But for those who haven't benefited, the insanity of the current order has always been obvious. In an apocalyptic age, this insanity begins to become apparent to all, even though there is a great deal of psychic resistance.

While religion has been considered a conservative force for many, the truth is more nuanced. It is indeed true that religions have often been the preserver of traditional ways and values. But religion has also often been a subversive force, challenging the status quo and undermining traditional values.

It is an oft-repeated truism that, while different religions may indeed be different, they are all about the same god—"many paths to the same summit", or something like that. But what if, one might ask, there is no single god? What if there are different summits and different truths, even contradictory ones? What if an age of interfaith spirituality is opening us up to the possibility not of a single answer but a web of paradoxical questions?

These questions are answered best with further questions, questions that cannot be asked through the logic of either/or. It requires a spirituality of both/and—the spirituality of the Trickster.

As Lewis Hyde[31] and other scholars have noted, there is much that has been lost in the monotheistic project, particularly in its rejection of the Trickster. Its more dualistic expressions have turned the Trickster into the devil, turned the necessary work of paradox, foolishness, and insanity into something forbidden or evil. This is a major reason why religion is so easily condemned by progressives—because the only religion we hear of seems so inflexible. Ironically, the black-and-white rejection of religion promulgated by the secular left is merely another side of this dualistic worldview.

Indeed, even when we think we've embraced a new paradigm through the interfaith axiom "many paths to the same summit," the Trickster subverts that paradigm, too, revealing to us a radically pluralistic world filled with paradox.

Most fundamentally, the Trickster is a boundary crosser. Culture functions through the construction of boundaries: we learn, through the stories of our religious traditions, what is sacred and profane, appropriate and inappropriate. There are good reasons for this, of course. Civilization provides some stability and order in a chaotic and wild world. A healthy fear of the wild is not such a bad thing. But too much rejection of the wilderness can lead to a rejection of our own wildness, the source of our creativity. The Trickster dances at the edge between the clean and the dirty. He shakes us up, calling upon us to question those categories.

American racial categories demonstrate the absurdity of society's categories and boundaries. Created during the early years of the trans-Atlantic slave trade in North America, American racial categories arbitrarily divided Americans into two categories—black and white. In addition to serving the purpose of justifying slavery, these categories were fundamentally religious in nature, based upon the radical dualism of Calvinism. Whiteness was associated with purity and salvation; blackness was tainted, subhuman and damned, which is why the so-called "one-drop" theory—in which one "drop" of African blood defined a person as black—persists.

The Trickster can appear to be the fool. He is wildly inappropriate. He shows us the absurdity of the inertia of our well-worn paths. Similarly, the Trickster behaves like a child. His inappropriateness is not unlike the way a child might behave. And it is the retention of our child-like qualities—called "neotony" by biologists—that give us our most human of attributes, our desire to explore and create. These are the qualities that allowed us to become human, to venture out of the forests and into the unknown savannahs and beyond.

Trickster has no place. Lacking the wisdom of other species, Raven and Coyote must figure out how to survive by their wits—just like the human. But it is this very lack of in-born wisdom that allows for the process of self-discovery, creativity, and world-building to occur. In our cities today, coyotes thrive, carving out niches that are only possible because of their radical adaptability. Much like the human, they thrive not because they are the fastest or strongest predator, but because they can remake and re-imagine themselves.

In this way, the Trickster tale is also a Creation Story. The trickster makes and re-makes our world by shaking things up, by unbalancing things. While most of the gods provide stability, the Trickster destabilizes. Similarly, we understand from modern science that too much stability is stagnancy, even death. The Trickster engages in the dance of predator and prey, allowing for Creation to occur again and again, for the Universe to evolve and unfold.

In dualistic monotheism, the Trickster was turned into the devil. Religion, in such theologies, serves the purpose of separating saved and damned. Trickster becomes the violator of these limits. All this is not to say that the tendency of religions and cultures to make order of our world is not important and necessary. Of course it is. But the Trickster reminds us that we cannot become too attached to any order—even a good one. Even one that says "God is One." All cultures require, paradoxically, the creative tension between cultivating a sense of belonging on one hand, and the undermining of boundaries on the other. It is not that God is *not* "one"—rather, God is both one and many. The absurdity of this paradox lies at the heart of the healthy approach to interfaith spirituality that not only accepts but also embraces the wild and paradoxical world in which we live.

Healthy boundaries, of course, are an important part of any culture and, indeed, any psyche. A culture whose boundaries are too rigid is fascist; a culture without any order or boundaries is one in which no one knows her place. As Yeats puts it, "the center cannot hold." And we've all known people so rigid they cannot function outside of their comfort zone, just as we know those without healthy boundaries—and the neurotic and dysfunctional behavior that results. It is a balance between cosmos and chaos that the Trickster navigates. This navigation is particularly poignant in apocalyptic times, when the blurred lines of culture and cosmos become apparent to all. The insanity of the Trickster, in such times, is the only thing that makes sense.

* * * * *

If one had spent much time in a Christian church, one might get the sense that Jesus was a white pastor from a suburb of Cleveland, clean cut and wearing a tie, warning us to obey authority. The difficulty with talking about the historical Jesus is that he has become, in the collective religious imagination, more God than man. And, of course, the trouble with talking about God is that we project onto God our own fears, beliefs, and ideas. How else could God support both the civil rights movement and the KKK? But perhaps it would more accurate to say that Jesus supported those movements–at least according to their adherents. For it was not the Jewish peasant from Galilee, the Jesus of history, that is usually referred to, but Jesus Christ.

Context is everything. When we understand the context of a historical figure we are able to interpret his words and deeds in a way that makes sense. It is not that the life of Jesus doesn't have anything to teach us about our lives today; rather, it is that by de-contextualizing his life, by acting as though Jesus was a white guy living in a subdivision in Ohio, we fail to see what Jesus even meant then, and miss the opportunity to apply his story to our own times.

Reza Aslan, in his recent book *Zealot*,[32] argues that Jesus was a threat to both the imperial authorities from Rome and the religious authorities of the Temple. Jesus fit clearly into the movement known as the zealots, messianic figures who aimed to undermine the unholy alliance between Rome and the Temple. In fact, there is only one reason Jesus would have been crucified according to Roman law: for sedition.

Aslan provides many examples of how we have failed to understand Jesus by failing to recognize context. When Jesus says, "render unto Caesar what is Caesar's; render unto God what is God's" he is not simply saying that we should go ahead and pay the tax because it has nothing to do with God anyway. He is undoubtedly referring to the fact that the land is God's, not Rome's. *Yes,* he is saying, *we can pay this tax. Why not? But Rome should give the land back to the people.* Landless peasants like Jesus would have been trapped in cycles of debt and poverty—the emphasis on the notion of "debt forgiveness" in the scriptures makes subtle reference to this; it is not merely about "sin" (see chapter 4). Forced to go to the cities for work, they would then be confronted with Roman power, Hellenistic culture, and Jews who had turned their backs on the poor. Render unto God, indeed.

The reasons we fail to recognize Jesus for who he most likely was—a radical Jewish peasant who challenged the authority of his day and the values they represented resulting in his execution for sedition—are rooted in the evolution of Christianity, the writings of

Paul and the politics of his time and place. Paul had developed a theology that turned Jesus into a god, that ignored his actual life, and that sought to open the gospel to non-Jews. After the destruction of the second temple, these ideas caught on as Jews and Christians were spread throughout the empire and urbanized. No longer were the concerns of the Galilean peasantry at the forefront; the new Christians were increasingly urban and gentile. Mystery cults, less concerned with the specific interests of marginalized peoples and more interested in individual salvation that could be applied universally, became increasingly popular with the urban classes. Moreover, there was an interest, after the destruction of the Temple and the banishment of the Jews from Palestine, in distancing the emergent Christian movement from anything Jewish. Understanding this fact can help to unpack much of the tendency of the scriptures to downplay Jesus' opposition to Rome and overstate the role of "the Jews" in his downfall.

While Aslan's argument that Jesus would have advocated land rights for his people is hard to refute, there is also the deeper issue that I think runs throughout the synoptic gospels. Jesus' teaching is so radical it is apocalyptic: the values of the old world must be turned upside down. He did not merely want a more just world; he wanted a re-imagined one.

* * * * *

The question I would pose for Christians today is what is the nature of this re-imagined world? While it is possible that Jesus, like other Zealots, advocated an armed rebellion and an earthly kingdom, there is also much evidence from his teachings that he advocated neither a worldly kingdom nor a wholly transcendent one. That is, he promoted a more just order, a radically changed world, but seemed also to believe we could arrive at it through means far different from his contemporaries.

First, Jesus was part of the apocalyptic movement. Unlike Paul, he seemed not to believe that the "end" would arrive at some specific point in the coming days but that it was already here if we can only undergo an interior transformation. This concept, called "realized eschatology", represents a unique teaching that likely came from the historical Jesus.

Second, Jesus refers to himself not as a God, but as "son of man". The meaning here is contested and complex, but it seems to mean that he was (a) a human being, not a god, and (b) engaged in the mystical practice known as *Merkabah*.[33] Jesus was no different from any other human being, but he communed with the divine without the mediation of the temple. This would have been a radical and threatening practice indeed.

Finally, in breaking bread with the untouchables of his society, Jesus ushered in a new sacrifice: this is where the communion ritual comes from. It required no priest—at least until the church was Romanized.

The story of Jesus remains incredibly influential today. The reclamation of the Jesus of history could teach us so much about our world today, more than much of the teachings we find in the Church: he was a poor man from a marginalized class, forced to sell his labor because of the policies of the empire; he challenged that empire, demanding that they deal honestly with the fact that they'd stolen the land of his ancestors; and he challenged his own people, who struggled to retain their identity and to find meaning in the face of cultural imperialism. For Christians, seeing the historical Jesus in context should not hinder their experience of Jesus the Christ; rather, in understanding more deeply who Jesus likely was, the experience of Jesus Christ through the engagement of the believer in the world makes for a more alive, more meaningful, more authentic Christianity. In other words, don't look to find Jesus in the eyes of the preacher at your megachurch; find him in the undocumented laborer, standing by the side of the road, waiting for work to feed his family. This man, like Jesus, is living at the edge, and can see the injustice and the apocalyptic nature of the day.

Many, throughout history, have understood this. When Dr. Martin Luther King, Jr. said that, "Human salvation lies in the hands of the creatively maladjusted," he was linking the experience of his people, an oppressed and enslaved people, to the Israelites in bondage and to the Jews of Roman Palestine. He called on his people not to adjust to the injustice of his day. He saw that much of the "maladjustment" to an unfair and insane world—and the laws of Jim Crow were truly insane—was a rational response. What was required was to turn one's maladjustment into something creative and transformative.

* * * * *

While it is often suggested that the prophetic traditions of the monotheistic religions are more conducive to political change and that the "Eastern" religions are more internal, it is also true that there is a deeply countercultural streak in many Eastern traditions. Lao Tzu, for example, and the Taoist sages who followed him, called upon people to overturn the values of their day. Softness overcomes the hard, he taught, and we should act not through straightforward aggression, but through *Wu Wei,* the harmonious act of allowing the cosmos guide us toward change.

So, while this may appear to the Modern mind as mere passivity, what it actually teaches us is to act in ways that turn our world upside down, ways that are so radical and countercultural they undermine more profoundly than the militant the values of a society. This upside-down-ness—"the first shall be last"; "love your enemies"—while often appearing to be passive, is fundamental to apocalyptic revolution and to the countercultural aspect of the spirituality that arises from it.

* * * * *

We find ourselves at another edge. An apocalyptic moment. Adherence to the values of our culture lead us on the path of destruction. To be clear, I refer to the culture of global Capitalism that dominates the planet at this time. This is a culture that treats the Earth as a machine and individuals as isolated consumers in competition with one another. A boundary must be crossed. It seems simple to many. We possess the scientific knowledge and the technological skills to overcome the ecological crisis. But somehow we do not change. For we have not yet exposed the insanity of our current system. As Dr. King was trying to tell us, we should appear to be crazy, at times, in the face of an unjust, insane system. This is the work of the artist, the work of the rebel, and the work of the Trickster, breaking down barriers and shattering cosmos and cosmology. It is the work that Jesus did when the heavens split open upon his birth and when he chased the moneychangers out of the Temple—two acts of apocalypse that must be seen as linked. Such work can be dangerous, even foolhardy. But at this moment, it is also necessary.

Chapter 9

Religion at the End of Religion

It is perhaps unavoidable that a side effect of globalization and the information age is the emergence of interfaith spirituality. In part, the interfaith movement arises out of a normal human response to being connected—both through access to information and to interaction with people—to an unprecedented number of traditions and philosophies. But this is not entirely new; human beings have always integrated their own traditions with the new beliefs they have encountered. Just look at the syncretism of West African religions with Catholicism in the emergence of Santeria and Candomble or the integration of Taoism and Buddhism to give rise to Chan/Zen Buddhism.

But there is something new about both the scale and the significance of what is happening in today's interfaith movement. For one, there is a conscious effort to embrace a new kind of spirituality. This spirituality differs from previous forms primarily in that it isolates the believer. There is no more cultural context; rather, the radically individualized seeker can simply choose what to believe. She is at once alone and free.

At the same time, there is no other alternative to interfaith. The old churches are dying or are mired in fundamentalism. An interfaith spirituality is the only way to approach spirituality, and this approach reflects some of the core elements of the apocalyptic nature of our day. If one thinks of religion in the way that most do—participation in a rigid tradition—we may have reached its end. At the same time, human beings have no less need for the role that religion plays in our lives, for the stories it tells. We must ask, therefore, what is the role for religion at the end of religion?

* * * * *

One of the great challenges for anyone active in the interfaith movement is how to articulate exactly what something so inherently diverse is all about. Generally speaking, interfaith groups fall into one of two categories—both of which, we shall see, are inadequate in a holistic re-imagining of the world in the context of apocalypse.

Interfaith or, perhaps more accurately, interspirituality, is a wonderful, beautiful, radical idea. But we are in need of going deeper. There is a risk that in claiming to be all things interfaith ends up mired in superficiality. The interfaith movement has a crucial role at this moment in history, a moment which I describe as apocalyptic.

* * * * *

PART OF THE BEAUTY of a concept like interfaith is its diversity. I've noticed that the term means something slightly different to everyone. As a way of talking about the subject, I have created some general categories. These are not meant to be definitive, but to provide a means of having a discussion about how one might speak about interfaith meaningfully. We could look at the categories as the two poles of the movement, the extremes toward which most interfaith institutions gravitate.

The first category I would describe as secular. Groups in this category are interested in dialogue across faiths, but not in the depth of these faiths. Common ground is found, but only in secular areas. Generally, this group is wary of interfaith groups or philosophies that claim to find any spiritual unity or ultimate truth across faiths. Most frequently this category can be associated with various interfaith organizations that attempt to foster religious "tolerance".

The second category holds that there is indeed a spiritual connection among the faith traditions. But whereas the first group is often far too intellectual, the second tends to be anti-intellectual. I call them New Age Fundamentalists because, like fundamentalists of the great faiths, they reduce the answer to every question to a simple phrase, rejecting the beautiful, chaotic diversity of our religious world. Moreover, the soul—i.e., the isolated, Cartesian soul—not the world, is the focus. There is a certain self-indulgence in this approach, a fixation on healing the soul, a soul that is entirely apart from what is happening in the world. While the New Age Fundamentalist, like any fundamentalist, claims to draw from an ancient wisdom, only in the hyper-individualized Modern world could such an approach even exist.

The most of obvious critique of the secular interfaith movement ironically comes from the very group that birthed it: academia. Most academics rightly criticize the anti-intellectualism and cultural appropriation of the New Age Fundamentalist. In doing so, they ignore what their own scholarship tells us about the nature of religion: that our religions have never been static and isolated. There has always been an effort to integrate the philosophies of various traditions. As mentioned above, one needs only to look at the syncretism of African religions and Christianity in the New World; or the blending of Greek and Jewish traditions at the birth of Christianity; or the integration of northern European traditions and Christianity as it spread across Europe; or the Taoist and Confucian influence on Zen; or the Hindu influence on Buddhism, Jainism, Sikhism, and Indian Islam. I could go on.

At the same time, reducing the world's religions to oversimplified platitudes often reflects a poor understanding. To be an adherent of a faith means more than liking a couple of ideas, more than changing one's clothes. It means inhabiting a new world. To have any clear understanding of how the world's religions truly do reflect a shared, integral wisdom—not to mention avoiding a shallow and offensive appropriation—one must understand the underlying cosmology, the essential context in which they arise.

* * * * *

Each group, while seemingly quite different, actually reflects the same worldview—that is, the fragmentation, literalism, and individualism of the Modernity. The first group is fragmented and literal in keeping with the Western intellectual tradition. Each religion is distinct and separate and we should keep it that way, the logic goes. The second, while appearing to reject Modernity—again, this is just like the fundamentalist—actually retains the core values of the Modern industrial world: the distinct, separate, isolated individual. The soul, in this approach, is entirely separate from the world. In each case, the Modern industrial world's core assumptions are retained: that each religion, each individual, is separate and isolated from one another.

Why does it matter? When the mythic edge of apocalypse is reached, the old way of doing things, the old consciousness, is overturned. Indeed, we have reached the edge of the Modern world. This apocalypse, like others before it, must involve a re-imagining of the relationship between the human and the world that is our home. The question for humanity at this moment is how this end is going to come about. Globalization and industrial Capitalism have brought us wealth and inequality, unprecedented individual rights and unprecedented destruction of the natural world. Will the end come with horrific death and destruction that seems imminent with global warming? Perhaps this is unavoidable. Certainly history has taught us that loss and despair will change one's way of relating to the world. But perhaps we can, in the midst of the despair that is surely a part of life, come to a richer, more enchanted, more meaningful worldview, one that allows us to participate in the rich tapestry of nature and humanity's diversity. For religion to play any role in the re-imagining, it can only do so if it embraces a both-and rather than an either-or consciousness. That is, interfaith spirituality cannot avoid certain contradictions because religions, on the surface at least, often contradict one another. But a great deal of the paradigm shift in which we find ourselves is about embracing the paradoxical nature of our world.

* * * * *

In order to become a viable religious expression in the post-apocalyptic, post-religious world, religion can participate in this paradigm shift in several ways.

First, it can reject the fragmentation of modernity in embracing the paradoxical nature of existence. To do this one must connect to the mystical elements of religion and to the nature-based traditions. The emerging interfaith spirituality cannot be found in avoiding the difficult questions. Our religious traditions are at once deeply interconnected and wildly diverse.

Second, we must understand the cosmologies and worldviews—that is, how a culture sees the relationship between the individual and the absolute—of the spiritual traditions in order to find a deeper, more authentic connection among them. While I do advocate an integral spirituality that sees where the religions interconnect, one must be careful to take a rigorous approach that acknowledges their genuine differences.

Third, we must embrace the insights of science, especially those that call into question the assumptions made in the Modern world. The both-and consciousness is indeed supported by many recent insights of science, whereas the either-or consciousness is a product of an obsolete, Newtonian scientific paradigm.

Fourth, we must express the new insights we have through creativity and imagination. For it is the mythic, not the logical—the Greeks would have called this *mythos* as opposed to *logos*—that expresses the core values of a culture.[34] In other words, our poets and story-tellers can make the insights of science come alive, and facilitate re-imagining.

* * * * *

When one studies the world's religions, a great deal of time is often spent on the various doctrines of the faiths. These are, of course, important. But we perhaps give them an undue amount of our focus. Modernity has taught us that information is the most important thing. In fact, when it comes to religion, it is the *story* that is paramount. Indeed, no religious tradition is without a myth. And it is the myth that invites us to participate in that reality, connecting our individual story to the greater one. The mythic is what brings the doctrine alive.

The myth is how the values of a tradition or culture are conveyed. I would argue that interspirituality as a way of seeing the world can be a part of the basis for a new myth. That is, the values of interspirituality speak to a world that is not fragmented, a world in which we can hold the paradox of two seemingly contradictory facts. If Modernity is marked by fragmentation and either-or logic, interspirituality is marked by integration and both-and, paradoxical thinking.

Additionally, interfaith movements can and must uphold certain values that speak to the specific struggles of this moment. I would describe these values as "cosmocentric", that is, values that connect us more deeply to the rhythms of the earth, to the story of the Universe, to our selves as expressions of the cosmos. For the apocalypse of this moment is the result of isolation from the community of life.

Moreover, we are each participating in the telling of this new myth as we tell our own stories. No individual can create the new myth. It comes together as a tapestry, a story made up of stories woven together. It is unlikely that a new myth will come from the elites alone. The wisdom of the margins is required.

This integration of a new story is how a new cosmology comes forth. In today's world, I believe that this new cosmology must integrate the insights of modern science with the wisdom of our mystical and philosophical traditions. Whereas the myth of Modernity was based on the notion of the Universe as a machine, the new myth must be of a sacred, organic Universe. Whereas the myth of Modernity was based on a fragmented world in which each of us is independent, the new myth must teach us that we are interdependent and interconnected. For me, the fundamental metaphor to build from is that of the Universe as our womb, and its unfolding a process of continual birthing.[35] This is the work of the mythmaker, the poet, the artist.

Thomas Berry calls the telling of this new story our "Great Work".[36] It is the task of mythmaking, of world-making, the most fundamental act of our humanity. The most ancient artwork, the cave paintings, reflected this: our ancestors, when they painted handprints on the walls of the cave, understood that we are always at the edge of our world, our womb, creating meaning.

These ancient paintings also commonly depict the relationship of predator and prey, the ecological reality that our ancestors deeply felt, that we have largely forgotten. Far from the rugged individualists that Modernity would have us to be, we are ecological beings, deeply interconnected to a community of living beings. The great predators from which we fled and the prey we chased on the African plain shaped our minds and our bodies, our communities and our stories.

The interfaith movement has always appreciated the desire for cultural diversity. But often it has lacked a real articulation of why diversity is so important. The importance of diversity—and of difference—is a lesson that ecology teaches us well. Whereas a loss of genetic diversity leaves gaps in the ecosystem that may not be filled, the loss of cultural diversity—for example, the loss of a spiritual tradition, a language, a culture—leaves us with a gap in the cultural ecosystem. Just as the loss of the wolf leaves the ecosystem imbalanced, so to does the loss of, say, feminist theology to provide a balance to patriarchy. This is only one example. We simply cannot say what kinds of worldviews might provide us with potential answers to the challenges our species faces. Just as a loss of genetic diversity leaves a species subject to disease, without a diversity of perspectives humanity might not survive.

* * * * *

Introduced at the right moment, a mere idea can become a movement. I believe that this is just such a time for interfaith. This moment—Modernity—is marked by many things that are coming to an end: fossil-fuel-based industry, individualism, Capitalism, imperialism. Above all else, this moment is about a loss of meaning, emptiness. But this void is pregnant. Apocalypse, after all, means "unveiling." We have the opportunity to make new worlds of meaning. Of the four suggestions above, it is the creative and imaginal which are most important. We must give birth, through our imaginative capacities, to a world in which spirituality, paradoxically, can represent the beautiful, chaotic diversity of humanity and be a source of our ultimate unity.

Chapter 10
The New Myth

"WHERE'S YOUR MOTHER?" my father asked, fumbling with his keys and, more significantly, his emotions. He couldn't bear to go inside to look for her. So I did. She stood in the kitchen, weeping, clutching the book.

"Are you having a hard time, mom?" I asked.

"It was his favorite book," she sobbed, showing me *Sylvester and the Magic Pebble*. I remembered the book well. It is the story of a donkey, Sylvester, who accidentally, magically, turns himself into a rock, and the year his parents spend looking for and mourning him before he finally, miraculously, returns. The book had always made her cry.

I held her for a while, sharing the unspoken knowledge that my brother would not return like Sylvester. "Come on," I said. "Let's go."

"I wanted to bury the book with him," she said.

"We can do that," I said. "It's OK."

And we got in the car—for the first time since my brother was born thirty-seven years before, a family of three—to bury my brother and his favorite book.

* * * * *

Books had always been important for us. Not only for my mother (a reading teacher) and me (a writer) but for my father and brother as well. I can see now, as a parent, how stories become the stuff that brings a world into being, the stuff that brings the individual into community. There was a little bit of Sylvester with my brother always—it made sense to bury the book with him. Books allow for the emerging interior self to connect to the broader world through space—in broadening one's sense of possibility and interrelatedness—and time, in connecting us to the stories of the past.

Even before there were books, human beings told stories. Before we spent our evenings around the light of the television, we sat around the fire. And we—not a box with a screen—told the stories. Storytelling was among the earliest art forms and, like all art forms, was participatory. The story comes into being not when the writer puts it on paper, but in the space in between reader and writer, between the teller and the listener. The participatory imagination of the audience co-creates it. And together, worlds are created. The oldest stories are stories of creation, stories that always end with the listener; for a creation story tells us not only about the cosmos beyond, but the cosmos within us, not only tells us the history of our world, but how we fit in it.

Telling stories, as much as anything else, makes us human. It is our especially human way of making a world.

* * * * *

There are no spiritual traditions I know of that do not revolve around stories. Students of religion and converts so often start in the wrong place, with philosophies and theologies, or worse, lists of rules. If you want to understand a spiritual tradition, the place to go is the story. For in the story, the hardest questions are asked: Who am I? Why am I here? Where are we going?

And stories, like faith traditions, are alive. We like to think of them as being one thing, written down at some point and never changing. But the truth is that what it means to be a Christian or a Jew or a Buddhist or a Hindu has been changing throughout history, and is always contextual. The apparent solidity of the written word belies the fact that the story evolves, too, even when the words on the page do not change. For contexts change, and with them, interpretations.

If we want to understand the Hebrew Bible, for instance, we are better off looking at the Exodus story than merely the Ten Commandments. In either case, there is a complex set of contexts the help bring the texts to life. Scholars can help us come to understand the historical context, of course. But it is the participation by the reader in the text that truly brings it to life: The captivity in Babylon has more meaning, and even new meaning, through the eyes of those in captivity, the migrants and the incarcerated; American Christianity only truly could understand the Exodus story through the eyes of Black America, a people who became a people in their yearning to be free.

These special stories are called "myths". Sadly, we've turned that word into an insult. It has become something like a synonym for a lie. But myths are simply stories that tell us something more important, more essential, than mere facts. They give us a sense of who we are and our place in the cosmos. They allow us to grapple with truths that are paradoxical and that aren't necessarily a matter of knowing information. Another way of putting it is to say that the myth is the primary way that a culture conveys a cosmology. And a cosmology is not merely about the Universe out there; it is about the Universe within. It links individual and whole.

The question we all have, I suspect, is not so much about what happens to us after we die but whether or not we are alone in the Universe. Are we participating in a community or not? Are we essentially interconnected or isolated? If we are alone, no afterlife we seek after would be worth much; for me, even a blink of an eye with the possibility of true communion with others would be preferable to such an eternity. And we are brought together by the story, the fabric of our social, cultural, and spiritual ecology.

* * * * *

"We are in trouble just now," writes Thomas Berry, "because we do not have a good story."[37] Berry is writing about industrial civilization and the story we have—told through the mechanisms of consumer Capitalism—that teaches us that our world is a "collection of objects"[38] to be exploited. It is the story that tells us we are fundamentally alone and in competition with one another, the story that we become who we are based on what we can buy. And the "trouble" he refers to is the imminent ecological, planetary collapse due to our overconsumption.

Neuroscience tells us that the story is the way we process and integrate information. Modern mass media saturates us with information, overwhelms us with it. We have nowhere to place it, no way to integrate it. This is one of the effects of the Tech Revolution. We are maladapted to process and integrate the narratives we digest today with the proliferation of mass media.

The work of making a myth, mythopoesis, is the work of making a world, a psychic world within each of us that is shared through culture. Symbolically, this world is conceptualized through the mandala, the map of the soul and the map of the world that is, essentially, the same—micro- and macro-cosm. Simply put, it answers the most fundamental of all questions: Who am I? The myth of Modernity—the story that Berry is suggesting isn't good enough—tells us that we are fundamentally consumers, defined by what we buy; that we are isolated individuals, separated from the web of life; and that we are part of a mechanistic, machinelike world.

There is no more important work than re-imagining

this story. And it is work that requires not merely the mind, but the whole self. It requires not merely an individual, but an entire culture. The new story will be more tapestry than a single cloth, more library than single text.

To bring forth a new myth requires work that is deep and hard. We must get outside and get our hands dirty to re-embed in the earth; we must explore our interior lives and do the soul-work that brings about the deepest insights; we must engage the old story with critical consciousness to become, in the Gramscian sense, philosophers for the people;[39] we must sing and dance and play and explore.

My suspicion is that the new story must come from the margins, from those who haven't been served by the story we have now. This was an insight that Jesus seems to have had. He didn't seek out the temple priests or the Greek elites or Roman power; rather, he went to those who were, as he was, at the margins of society. There was a wisdom from those margins that could not be found at the centers of power. Indeed, in today's world this would mean turning away from the university and looking to the streets, away from Wall Street and toward the shanty towns outside the centers of capitalist power. It means turning to the "creatively maladjusted", those who do not adapt to an insane world and instead attempt to re-imagine it. It is the kind of wisdom that the Trickster tales teach us: that there is an insanity in the work of building human civilization, and to appear mad in the face of it is a deeper wisdom than conforming to it.

But those at the margins, of course, are taught that they are there because of their own deficiencies. "Choices" is a word we will here over and over again in our poor schools, the schools that send more of our youth to prison than college—as if life were so simple, as if mere individual choices determine our fate and there is not a whole Universe of other choices conspiring to affect us as well. This is the *deficit narrative*. The reclamation of the narrative is the *counter-narrative*. This must be a central aspect of any worthwhile educational program for the marginalized. It was what Jesus and Chuang Tzu and Baal Shem Tov, to name a few, offered: A narrative that challenges the one we have been given.

And while it isn't my place to dictate what a new myth might be, I would make a few suggestions: It would be a story that speaks to the world not as machine but as living organism, a dynamic process of birthing. It would a story that speaks to our interconnectedness, privileging relationship over the individualism of Capitalism.

It is easy to see, I think, how a counter-narrative might be useful for the oppressed. But we must come to terms with the fact that the condescending term "at-risk", applied most to black and brown youth, applies to all of us. We are an at-risk species on an at-risk planet. Our work, our great work, is to tell a new story for us all. Anything less is the rearrangement of deckchairs on this planetary Titanic.

* * * * *

Apocalypse is the end of a story. It is the cultural moment when the old stories no longer speak to the people. It is the moment when new stories must be revealed, created. The new myth, therefore, is the product of the great re-imagining, the way to survive not only our physical peril, but also the spiritual peril of a life without the meaning that a good story provides.

* * * * *

We made it to the cemetery, and I stammered through the eulogy. My brother had little patience for intellectual and spiritual laziness and preferred to face the unknown with honest unknowing. Telling people what they want to hear makes a lot of money in the pulpit, but to honor my brother I had to tell another story: that life is hard, and short; even the luckiest among us gets a mere blink of an eye and cannot avoid suffering. It is funny that the stories of so many of our great spiritual icons—Jesus and the Buddha, for example—are stories of this encounter with suffering, and yet our religious institutions so often seek to avoid its reality.

I held my mother as she placed the book in my brother's grave. His sons stood uncomprehendingly in the face of eternity. It was autumn. For a moment, in the stillness of the cemetery, I could feel the movement of seasons. Off in the distance there was a high school. My brother had played football there once in high school, my mother said.

Like the seasons, stories bring us into participation with the cosmos. We will all die. My brother's ashes were placed in the earth like the bodies of his ancestors.

And like the seasons, stories come back. The spirits of our ancestors live on in story. They do not remain static. We can participate with stories, change them. They are there to serve us now and in the future. It matters less if Jesus said exactly the words written down in the

Bible than how those words come alive for us, make our lives meaningful, and, of course, what we do with those words. Words make worlds. And the mythology of my brother can be the way he remains with his sons in some small way.

Chapter 11
Science & Spirituality

I feel engulfed in the infinite immensity
of spaces whereof I know nothing
and which know nothing of me. I am terrified.[40]
–**Blaise Pascal**, *Pensees*

THE DISSOCIATION OF SCIENCE and spirituality is so thoroughly embedded in Modern consciousness that it seems like common sense. Those who would separate the two seem sober and rational, while those who conflate them often appear to be embarrassingly ignorant, making claims that suggest the Bible should be read literally and therefore the world is only a few thousand years old.

But the separation of these two areas is neither a given—for almost all of human history there was no separation between what we could observe about the natural world and our spiritual lives—nor is it necessarily a good thing. For, while it is surely better to separate the two than to take positions that, for example, deny climate change, we shall see that much is lost in their complete separation. Moreover, we shall also see that separating the two leads to a dissonance within each of us, a dissonance which brings us to the brink of apocalypse.

* * * * *

The categories of "Religion" and "Science" are products of Modernity. Fragmentation, and the placing of various aspects of life into different categories, is one of the hallmarks of Modern consciousness. Pre-modern culture would hardly have considered religion and nature as distinct categories; rather, they each would be woven into the whole fabric of life and world and worldview.

The separation of science and religion begins with the Modern period and the Protestant Reformation, which, for the first time, placed religion squarely in the realm of the private, the interior, the immaterial. The scientific method that emerged in the West would allow for unprecedented advances in knowledge about nature; but it arose within a particularly rigid religious culture and an emerging dualism between nature and spirit. All this would lead first to the conflicts between the Church and science—Galileo being the most prominent—and eventually to a compromise in mainstream Christianity that would lead to a grudging acceptance of science, but only insofar as it was not to influence theology.

This compromise was only a temporary fix. For it requires us to believe that the processes of our unfolding cosmos are in no way meaningful, in no way connected to the deepest mysteries of existence. The fundamentalist movement that has only grown in recent years is largely a response to this unsatisfactory solution. It sees the world in a way that is at once pre-Modern and, at the same time, profoundly Modern. Believing he is returning to the original intention of his religion, the fundamentalist holds that everything is a part of the unfolding mythic drama of his tradition. This is a pre-Modern view. At the same time, the fundamentalist can only exist in Modernity, for the fundamentalist can only understand that tradition *literally*, an approach that was unknown in the pre-Modern world.

We are left with scientists—not all, of course—who claim the world is meaningless, and fundamentalists who claim meaning is only found in the specific, literal interpretation of their tradition. For most of us, meaning must be found in personal things: family life, emotions, the arts. None of it has to do with the cosmos, with nature, with the world of which we are part.

As a result of this bifurcation, we have continued to devalue the natural world. Alienated from the cosmos, we have created a two-fold apocalypse: physically, because we do not believe that this world has any inherent value, we have continued to exploit and destroy. The fundamentalist can deny climate change because there is nothing sacred in nature. Even those who are not fundamentalists seem to believe this, for it lies at the center of Capitalism. As a result, we are precipitating the unparalleled destruction of the biosphere. And psychically, the devaluing of the cosmos requires us to want to move beyond it. Pie-in-the-sky Christianity is the individual version of this; apocalypse is the collective version. The fundamentalist yearns for the apocalypse, the complete eradication of the natural order, not for the prophetic work of creating a more just human order.

* * * * *

The Newtonian Universe is a cold one, a world in which matter moves predictably and mechanistically. The spiritual energy behind the cosmic spheres, described so beautifully by Dante as *amor*—love—was replaced with laws. It was also legalism, as opposed to traditional relationships, that opened the door for Capitalism. This has its benefits, especially with respect to individual rights. And, of course, there were many benefits to the discoveries of the Scientific Revolution. But humanity has also begun to discover that the truths uncovered in this period were, like all truths, incomplete. A new scientific revelation has occurred in which we have begun to rediscover the *organic* Universe—a cosmos that is an *evolutionary process* more than a machine.

It is important here to make a distinction between the deeper and more comprehensive sense of the word cosmology and the somewhat limited way it is used in science. A scientific cosmology describes the processes of the creation of the Universe. "The New Cosmology" refers to the Big Bang and evolutionary processes that have continued to occur since that moment. But a cosmology in the fullest sense requires a cultural narrative, a myth that is embedded into a culture to such a degree that it becomes a part of the consciousness of the people. A cosmology is about cosmos beyond and within. In this sense, the New Cosmology has not fully become a cosmology. For it has not yet been integrated. Our systems, our values and our cultural narratives all belong to the old cosmology, to the notion that the Universe is a machine and that we are mere parts.

* * * * *

Let us begin at the beginning. Of course, in a sense, there really is no beginning that one can distinguish from this moment. For the Universe is a seamless whole in time and space. All cosmologies offer a vision of the whole. What is included in a cosmology indicates what is real, what is sacred. The New Cosmology understands our Universe as a single event. And this word "event" is significant because it is a word that connotes time rather than space. There is no static, preexistent place that one might call the Universe; rather, the Universe is unfolding, time and space linked together as dimensions of the same seamless process.

So the Big Bang is happening now. It began, let's say, 13.7 billion years ago. But this was only the initiation of a process that continues. Where did the Universe originate? This is a trick question—for the Universe itself was contained in its entirety at a single point in the beginning. Its evolution has been the expansion of that single point. We were all there. It was here and in every other place in the Universe, admittedly in hotter and more crowded circumstances.

The single pointedness—the singularity—of our origins is significant. For this singularity will become a way to understand our end as well.

If our origins are everywhere, where is the edge of the Universe? Understood as process, the edge of the cosmos is not a place; rather, it is a time. And that time is now. Every moment, everywhere in the Universe, is the temporal edge of the Universe. Interestingly, this parallels what is called the realized eschatology of Jesus Christ. In certain Biblical passages (and in Gnostic texts like the Gospel of Thomas) Jesus, when asked about the end times, says that the end is happening now. He suggests that it is always happening, and it is a matter of perception. When we are able to transform our consciousness, the old world passes away and a new world is born.

* * * * *

In evolutionary cosmology, there is a repeated process of complexification and interiorization that gives rise to new singularities. Life began as a new singularity, a single cell from which all life evolved; each life, too, begins as a single cell, complexifiying and expanding. With this complexification comes a further process of deepening interiority or subjectivity. As new forms arise, they become microcosms, each containing the complexity and wisdom of the entire process of cosmic unfolding: planet Earth functions as a single whole, a microcosm, as does each ecosystem that arises on the planet.

Scientists talk of entropy, the notion that the Universe flows towards increasing disorder. The structure, for example, of the primordial singularity would have been simple and absolutely ordered. The unfolding cosmos seems to be a process of unfolding chaos. But at the same time, the Universe attains greater capacities for re-imagining itself and creating new forms of order and interconnection. The planet is born; the ecosystems come forth.

And now, human culture orders the Universe through the myth.

In the human, consciousness brings forth even further possibilities. If the end is everywhere (if we can only imagine it) then the imagination also allows one to create a new world. This is our edge; and it is also the newest singularity. This brings forth both promise and peril, possibility and despair.

* * * * *

According to the Sufi philosopher Ibn Arabi, the creation of the cosmos is the imagination of *Allah*. In the beginning, one might say, was *imagination*. All apocalypses are found in ends that are recapitulations of beginnings. The human imagination, the human soul, is a cosmos of imaginative possibility. And it is so to such an extent that the human possesses what one might call the ultimate delusion: loneliness.

The true end of the world for the human being is the belief that we are alone. We of course cannot be physically alone; but we can become psychically alone. In our isolation, our independence, we lose the connections that make us human. To stare at the screen, to lose the binds of culture and community, is to arrive at the apocalypse.

* * * * *

Integrating the principles of evolutionary cosmology into a re-imagined spirituality is not merely an intellectual exercise; it is essential if humanity hopes to have any kind of genuine spiritual life in the future. A culture cannot be bound together with this implicit agreement to segregate reality and spiritual life. For to do so leads inevitably to the unraveling of the real world—ecosystems are toxified; political systems are corrupted; the arts are trivialized and marginalized.

And we inhabit an absolute loneliness—isolated interior, psychic spaces.

Contemporary science is a revelation, and it reveals to us an organic Universe, one that is constantly birthing and revealing. It teaches us that we are intimately woven into the community of life and of cosmos. It teaches us that the Universe is process, not place, and that it is a single process. Its beauty is found in diversity, and at the same time, its sacredness is inescapable, for we are each other. The notion of separation is impossible.

Spiritually, these concepts allow us to see that our power, as humans, is not found in the degree to which we are separate from this process—this was the belief system that arose out of the inert and meaningless cosmos—but because we are participating in it. The human imagination is another phase in this cosmic process, unique but ultimately the same. But we must understand first what is the particular character of this emergent, imaginative singularity at this phase in cosmic unfolding.

Chapter 12
Singularity as Eschaton

ANY UNDERSTANDING OF THE END of the world can obviously only be imagined, and this process is limited by human experience. In other words, apocalypse is, by its very definition, about something beyond experience, beyond any context. Our description of it, therefore, is conditioned by the experiences we may have that can best approximate it. As discussed at the beginning of this book, there are those throughout history who have experienced apocalyptic episodes, events that involved the traumatic eradication of identity and culture. But even in the absence of such singular events, it is worth first briefly exploring what I will refer to as the emotions of apocalypse and the specific events that have been common in most or all of human experience. In understanding better the emotions behind such events, we can then explore that specific cultural singularities occurring on the planet today.

* * * * *

We all experience birth. Birth is the ultimate apocalypse, for the emergence from womb world to this world is the only exact correlation we have to the apocalypse. And while none of us remembers birth, many of us witness (or participate in) the birth of another. It leaves us utterly transformed.

We all experience death. It is perhaps just as appropriate a metaphor for apocalypse, seen from the other side. Many of our spiritual traditions understood this, and death was seen as a kind of birth. It is eradicating in a way that no other experience is. And the finality of watching a loved one die leaves us pondering the possibility of our own unavoidable death. Unlike birth, we encounter death aware and conscious, differentiated and, usually, attached to our individual existence. To part with this single life is the individual experience that parallels the collective experience of the eradication of a people—the apocalypse.

Sadly, war has also been a part of human existence for millennia. And there is perhaps no other experience that uproots us emotionally as war. For those who survive it, something in us tends to die through the experience of it. There is an impossible brutality that requires the shutting down of certain emotional parts of our selves. We let go of the stories in war and can only hope for a complete re-imagining. But the images of apocalypse are shaped by this brutality.

Finally, and perhaps more hopefully, there is the possibility that comes to life in falling in love. We destroy ourselves in love. We become new people. Worlds shatter. The hope is that we can embrace the notion that birth lies on the other side of death; and that it is the self-destruction of love, not war, that we should seek after.

* * * * *

As the previous chapter made clear, the edge of the cosmos is everywhere, at this moment. When a singularity is reached, the possibility of both the end of the old world and the birth of a new one is realized. This is true both in terms of the physical Universe as well as the psychic and spiritual one; it is true both of the world and of the worldview that we bring forth through our cultural traditions and mythologies.

Evolution can be understood as something that happens not merely physically, but also culturally. This does not mean that human culture is improving. Rather, that it is becoming more complex and diverse. In the journey of life on planet Earth, there is no improvement—the fly and oak tree and the human are all equally evolved. Each fills a certain role on the planet. But there have always been tipping points for life; cycles of mass extinction have occurred throughout Earth's history.

Humanity's communities have become increasingly complex as they have expanded and diversified. At the same time, in recent years, humanity has become increasingly homogenous. In this process, rather than connecting more deeply to the whole, individualism has increased. Interiority has deepened; but it has also isolated us. We find ourselves confronted with singularities that come in various forms.

* * * * *

We arrive at a spatial singularity through individualism. The story of Adam and Eve is informative here. It is not death per se that comes about in Adam and Eve's eating the fruit; it is that they now see themselves as individuals, with a separate consciousness. We become aware of our individual death, and begin to mourn and fear it. This story, told long before the comprehensive, individualistic, Modern consciousness emerged, shows that there was an intimation of such individualism present among our distant ancestors. And still, we remained embedded in community. The Israelites who told this story had no need for the afterlife; for their story was one of a people, a collective, a group that endures and for whom the sacred is found in their temple and on their land and among their shared traditions. It was the Greeks who brought to them—and to the emerging Christian tradition—the individualistic consciousness that was no longer satisfied by simply passing on our genes and our wealth and our wisdom to our descendants. "What happens to *me* when *I* die?" people began to ask.

In the Modern era, individualism increased exponentially. The American project is the pinnacle of the individualistic ethos. Americans believe that they have no history, no cultural traditions. They believe that they can simply choose. They believe that they are responsible for their fate.

The tech revolution has rapidly increased the rate at which individualism has intensified. We now interact with the world primarily through mediated and privatized spaces. There is no commons—rather, it has been replaced with a screen that has the illusion of a free and common space but is actually "enhanced" and individualized. It tracks our preferences and habits. In America, this is called freedom; in previous generations, this was called totalitarianism—an organizational structure from which there was no escape, in which participation is total and required. The difference, of course, is that we choose freely to participate in this structure. We believe that the old totalitarianism was different, believe that Mussolini and Hitler weren't welcomed as heroes by many.

Such technologies also lead us to the edge of the world in that they provide the ultimate fulfillment of the Manichean dream. Manicheanism, while originally referring to a specific, Gnostic religious group, refers more broadly to the philosophical dualism that has become a major aspect of Western philosophy. It originated with the Greeks and has been passed down through Christianity and, later, through the Newtonian-Cartesian paradigm, it became the default position of secular Capitalism. The world is not real; or at least it is absolutely separated from the disembodied life of the psyche. Technologies have moved us further and further from our bodies—the latest fantasy is that one can achieve eternal life as disembodied data. This, of course, assumes that the self is fundamentally disembodied information. It is a long-held value that has perhaps not been questioned enough. For we never had the opportunity to take it to its logical conclusion, which is that existence would be desired or even possible in the absence of a material world. It also fails to question what then happens to us and to our world when we take these values and beliefs to their logical extreme. It is the absurdity of the absence of an embodied life and the rejection, neglect and destruction of the natural, material world. This, we have been led to believe, is freedom—freedom from our imperfect, painful bodies and from the uncertainty of nature.

As stated in previous chapters, the ultimate end of freedom of this kind is loneliness. The singularity of individualism is the loneliness of a life lived as an absolute individual, disconnected from community.

* * * * *

We arrive at a temporal singularity through the end of progress. Progress, like individualism, is part and parcel of Modernity. Throughout the Modern period, an absolute belief in progress would have been a given. Few would have questioned the perpetuity or value of progress. We will always progress and improve; the new is always better than the old. It is not difficult to see how these values are woven into Capitalism, a system that depends upon and encourages endless growth and expansion.

But the end of the Modern era has brought about both the questioning of progress as a value and also of actual progress in real and measureable ways. First, we must come to terms with the finite and spherical nature of our planet. We are running out of room to grow, of spaces in which to expand. Real growth has slowed or stopped both economically and demographically. And this is a good thing considering the ecological impact of growth. But this is at odds with a cultural value system that has taught us that growth is a constant and beneficial aspect of our world.

For example, there is an assumption that technologies will always improve our world. We bring new technologies into our lives without question. Some seem to be obvious benefits. But even those can prove problematic. For example, the antibiotics that have saved millions of lives also put us in jeopardy. Others seem harmless and fun, like smart phones. But when we adopt them without limitation, they can do unexpected harm. And still others seem so obviously harmful that they would only be adopted by a sick species, determined to destroy itself, determined to bring about the apocalypse. Or, perhaps, a species so immersed in the mythology of progress that we are blind to the dangers. Only in such a culture would a people build a nuclear weapon.

So, as progress ends, or as our blind adherence to the myth of progress ends, we come to a singularity in time. The end of time's steady flow, in our cultural mythos, toward improvement. There is so much that cannot grow forever; and at this moment, we are confronted with this stark reality.

* * * * *

The spiritual singularity is reached through a loss of meaning. When the old stories no longer tell us who we are or provide us with a place in the world, we are lost and alone. Crisis turns to apocalypse; for we no longer have the psychic skills to cope.

Meaning is found, in the Modern world, in an entirely individual way. And this is a good thing, to an extent. It is a gift that one can read and explore the world to find one's own meaning in it, without relying solely on traditional values or the mediation of institutions. But the risk of Modern spirituality has always been that in its individualization, in its psychologization, it loses its ultimate purpose: to help us to find our place in the community of things and beings, to help us to locate the sacred within and beyond and, ultimately, to eradicate the artificial barrier between the two.

It is worth noting that spiritual singularity has nothing to do with individuality and plurality. These things are part of a healthy and evolving world. Diversity is good, as we could see in the discussion on ecology and wildness. The issue is whether or not we—unique individuals, all of us, either way—are ultimately alone.

* * * * *

IMAGINE WHAT IT WOULD be like to be the last person in the world who spoke your mother tongue. This seems unimaginable, but it is in fact a common occurrence in human history. Languages usually come and go naturally as they evolve. Other times, a people is eradicated, usually due to colonialism. When native peoples in the

New World encountered Europeans, many languages were lost due to a combination of brutality and exposure to germs from which they had no immunity.

A language is a uniquely human way of perceiving the world. The way we process all of the information we receive comes through our language. The way we find community comes through our language. While there is surely meaning and value and sacredness beyond language, it seems impossible for the human to have a fully enriching life in the absence of a shared language. To become the last speaker of a language is a profound experience of apocalypse. For it is to be truly alone, truly without a shared sense of meaning and purpose in the world.

In today's world, languages are disappearing like species, and with them, unique ways of understanding our world. And there are elders, alone somewhere, their children having gone to the city or abroad in search of work, their peers having died, who experience this singularity.

* * * * *

The three singularities of Modernity leave us at the point of apocalypse. We experience, through them, the trauma of death and of war. And the crisis of absolute loneliness felt by the last speaker in the world. The question is not whether these ends are coming. They are unavoidable. The question is what new world is birthed from these singularities.

Epilogue

An Imaginal Revelation

This is what you shall do: Love the earth and the sun and the animals, despise riches, give alms to every one that asks, stand up for the stupid and the crazy, devote your income and labor to others, hate tyrants, argue not concerning god, have patience and indulgence toward the people, take off your hat to nothing known or unknown, or to any man or number of men—go freely with powerful uneducated persons, and with the young, and with mothers of families—re-examine all you have been told in school or church or in any book, and dismiss whatever insults your own soul; and your very flesh shall be a great poem, not only in its words, but in the silent lines of its lips and face, and between the lashes of your eyes, and in every motion and joint of your body... The known Universe has one complete lover, and that is the greatest poet."

–Walt Whitman, 1855 Preface to *Leaves of Grass*[41]

Apocalypse is an act of the human imagination. It is so easy to forget that; for we inhabit a literal worldview, and impose literal thinking on even something as profoundly mythic as apocalypse. When we think of apocalypse, we also only think of the destruction, of what dies. We forget that apocalypse is revelation. Something is being born. Just as, for Ibn Arabi, the creation of the cosmos was an act of divine imagination, so too is the apocalypse an act of human imagination. It is the moment when we can re-imagine the world, re-create the world. It is the moment of revolution—not the revolution that replaces the one form of oppression with another and places a new group on the top of the hierarchy; rather, it is the revolution that turns the world upside down, the first becoming last.

* * * * *

Apocalypse is a rite of passage. For millennia, we have watched our children come into the world and cut the umbilical cord, recognizing that this is an act that has repeated itself and will repeat itself countless times: From singularity, new forms arise that become separate from the mother who birthed them. Paradoxically, this very insight teaches us that we never really are separate.

Our shamans learned to break through the cosmic barrier to a reveal new ways of understanding our place in the Universe. And we celebrated the passage of time—birth, coming of age, death—with our rites of passage celebrations. In the apocalyptic moment, we experience a collective re-birth, a collective rite of passage. We break through the cosmic barrier to uncover a new cosmology, a new consciousness.

* * * * *

Like all births, this one has the seeds of both beauty and trauma. Destruction and creation come together. Psychic and physical transformation cannot be entirely separated. The Earth dies along with the human heart. And so, we experience the end of both world and worldview, cosmos and cosmology. The inner and the outer cannot be separated.

The edges that we have reached are manifold. Our technologies and our economy have brought us to the singular loneliness of the ultimate abstraction. We seek after salvation in the form of information-based technologies, unaware that this is no solution, but the ultimate consequence of an old dream of Manichaean alienation from body and Earth. Replacing authentic relationship with information, we find ourselves at the edge of not merely loneliness, but also of a psychic alone-ness that is absolute—a singularity.

Capitalism's voraciousness has led us to another abyss. We run out of resources and peoples to exploit, so we privatize our own culture. As a consequence, we have threatened our wilderness, inhibiting our own wildness; we have destroyed the biodiversity upon which our ecosystems depend, leading to a diminishment of the cultural diversity on the planet. Globalization leads us on a path to realize that absolute singularity of our planet: It is a circle, another Easter Island.

Our planet, the biosphere, relies on biodiversity to remain viable. The human requires cultural diversity to remain viable. We risk reducing humanity to a single, global, Capitalist culture, a culture of abstract disembodiment and individualism; we risk reducing the planet to a paved, anthropocentric space. This is the dream of our culture—the *telos* towards which we strive. Its only result is apocalypse. Death—and a rebirth that is possible only with the imagination.

* * * * *

In astrophysics, a singularity is represented by a black hole. It is the loneliest place in the cosmos, a single point of such gravity that nothing can escape from it. Astrophysicists understand them only in theory, for they are impossible to visit, or even to see. One theoretical notion about them is that at the end of the black hole, the point of singularity, is a "white hole", the Big Bang of the birth of an alternate Universe.

And so, the psychic singularities of human-Earth apocalypse can also bring forth "Big Bangs". And humans create worlds through symbolic language, through art, through stories. We create new myths as new worlds. The most pressing question, for us all, is what is the mytho-poetics of this moment? What is the new story we must tell about who we are and our place in the cosmos? The revelation of this apocalypse does not come from beyond; it comes from us.

* * * * *

The role of imagination must be prominent in any apocalyptic vision; for it is, by definition, unknowable beyond the veil of the cosmos. Our earliest human ancestors distinguished themselves as mammals who could care for one another, who could build community, but also, most significantly, who could imagine a world into being. Imaginal worlds, mythic worlds, were created and co-created, imagined and re-imagined as we sat, for millennia, under the stars. But slowly, we moved from the mytho-poetic consciousness to the literal. This is a journey that has its roots in the earliest days of Western civilization.[42] The challenge is that getting to the other side of the veil, where a mytho-poetic consciousness resides, requires that very mytho-poetic consciousness.

And what would this new mythos look like? Although we cannot know for certain, we can imagine it. And, in some cases, we can even remember it; for there are elements of the new mythos that are as old as the cave paintings.

First, we must journey from abstraction to embeddedness. The Earth is dying; and it is largely dying due to our alienation from her and the natural processes of which we are a part. Our economic system and its values are dependent upon and reinforce those values—of abstract economies and disembodied individuals. The new mythos must remind us to feel the texture of the world, and to be a part of that world again. To taste the wind and the rain, to get our hands dirty and to see ourselves, again, as ecological beings.

This requires the journey from the mechanistic to the organic. We know, already, that the dualistic and mechanist view of the world is part of a worldview and a science that—while not exactly wrong—was incomplete. To see the world as machine is useful for an economy of extraction and exploitation, but it ultimately leads to our demise. The organic world, the world of our ancestors, allows us to experience the world holistically rather than dualistically.

All these mean that we experience our world as self, and our selves as the world. Within us is the entire cosmos. There is no such thing as the individual self; and the individualism of Modernity has led us to the brink of apocalypse.

Although some may think the use of apocalyptic language to describe this moment in human history is hyperbolic or alarmist, I would suggest that what I am offering is rather mild. Our situation is dire; only a thorough, worldwide revolution could break the spell of consumption that has led us to our destructive patterns. The prescription I am offering does not involve military action or a violent revolution. Rather, I am suggesting that something deeper is required, a changing of the patterns in our way of life and in our worldview. This transformation must be a spiritual revolution. But it is one that is so thorough that it even transforms what we mean by spiritual.

We can only approach this edge with an honest unknowing—to pretend otherwise is to court the hubris that has brought with it so much trouble in the first place. But we must also do so with a sense of genuine power. Not the power of false and shrunken egos that need to own a world that they cannot feel a part of, but the power of people who bring with them an entire cosmos of wisdom, the power of a people who come from the stars and can make worlds with their words, their minds, their hands. At the edge of the world, we must find also the courage to leap into the abyss, knowing that there is no alternative but to be reborn.

End Notes

1. *Selected Poems and Two Plays of William Butler Yeats*, ed. M.L. Rosenthal (New York: MacMillan, 1962) p. 91

2. Luke 17: 20-21

3. Mark 1: 14

4. Originally published in *Handprints on the Womb*

5. Carl Jung, "The Undiscovered Self," *Civilization in Transition*, Collected Works 10, par.585, quoted in Edward Edinger, *The Christian Archetype: A Jungian Commentary on the Life of Christ* (Toronto: Inner City Books, 1987) p.13

6. Theodore Richards, *The Conversions* (Stonington, CT: Homebound Publications, 2014) p.154

7. *The Collected Poems of Wendell Berry* (New York: Counterpoint, 1998) p.30

8. Mary Oliver, *New and Selected Poems: Volume One* (Boston: Beacon Press, 1992) p. 94

9. Nafeez Ahmed, "NASA funded study: industrial civilization headed for 'irreversible collapse'", *The Guardian,* March 14, 2014 accessed February 1, 2016, http://www.theguardian.com/environment/earth-insight/2014/

mar/14/nasa-civilisation-irreversible-collapse-study-scientists

10. Ibid

11. Ibid

12. David Abram. *The Spell of the Sensuous: Perception and Language in a More-Than-Human World.* (New York: Vintage Books, 1996)

13. Richards, *The Conversions*, p.172-173

14. In the infamous "Citizens United" case, the Supreme Court upheld the dubious legal fiction that corporations are legal "persons".

15. For more on mass incarceration, see Michelle Alexander's *The New Jim Crow: Mass Incarceration in the Age of Colorblindness* (New York: The New Press, 2012)

16. This little known fact is eerily reminiscent of the notorious three-fifths compromise, in which a slave was counted as three-fifths of a person calculating representation for slave states.

17. I am referring here exclusively to migrants who have left due to economic conditions, not to political refugees or those who have left countries afflicted with war.

18. David Indiviglio, "How Americans' Love Affair with Debt Has Grown", *The Atlantic*, September 26, 2010

19. Matthew 6:12

20. Luke 6:20

21. For more on the problems of the abstract economy, see Franco “Bifo” Berardi’s The Uprising: On Poetry and Finance (New York: Semiotext(e), 2012)

22. Ibid

23. See Thomas Picketty’s *Capital in the 21st Century* (Cambridge, MA: Belknap Press: 2014)

24. Ibid

25. For more on the extent of pollution from factory farms, see the Natural Resources Defense Council: http://www.nrdc.org/water/pollution/ffarms.asp

26. Wendell Berry, “The Pleasures of Eating,” *What Are People For?* (New York: Northpoint Press, 1989)

27. While it may be the case that much of what Plato attributes to Socrates is actually Plato, I suspect that this is authentic Socrates. For it seems that much of what he warns against is present in Plato’s later work. See *The Phaedrus.*

28. Go to www.chicagowisdomproject.org for more information

29. These metaphors are explored more comprehensively in my book *Creatively Maladjusted: The Wisdom Education Movement Manifesto* (Danvers, Mass.: Hiraeth Press, 2013)

30. William Ayers, *Teaching Toward Freedom: Moral Commitment and Ethical Action in the Classroom* (Boston: Beacon, 2004) p.48
31. See Lewis Hyde's *Trickster Makes This World* (New York: Farrar, Straus and Giroux, 1998)
32. Reza Aslan, *Zealot: The Life and Times of Jesus of Nazareth* (New York: Random House, 2013)
33. See Bruce Chilton's *Rabbi Jesus: The Jewish Life and Teachings that Inspired Christianity* (New York: Image Books, 2000)
34. For more on the mythos/logos dichotomy in the history of theological thought, see Karen Armstrong, *The Case for God* (Anchor, 2010)
35. Theodore Richards, *Cosmosophia: Cosmology, Mysticism, and the Birth of a New Myth* (Danvers, MA: Hiraeth Press, 2011)
36. Thomas Berry, *The Great Work: Our Way into the Future* (Broadway, 2000)
37. ibid
38. ibid
39. Ayers, *Teaching Toward Freedom* (Boston: Beacon, 2004) p. 101
40. Blaise Pascal, *Pensees* (London: Printed for Jacob

Towson, 1688), microform, III, 206.
41. Walt Whitman, *Specimen Days and Collect* (Brooklyn: Melville House Publishing, 2014) p. 311
42. See Plato's *Phaedrus*

Acknowledgements

Thank you to my wife, Arianne Richards, for her patience and courage; to my parents for all their support over the years; and to my people in Chicago for coming together to create this miracle called community when we need it most.

Thank you to Homebound Publications and to my editor and co-conspirator, Leslie M. Browning, for believing in this project; to Matthew Fox, Bill Ayers, Kurt Johnson and Gint Aras for your generous reading and feedback; and to my friends, colleagues and teachers at CIIS and FICS for providing fertile ground to grow these ideas.

And because a book is never a mere individual enterprise, but something that requires a web of connections extending into the past and throughout the world, I thank the ancestors and the youth of The Chicago Wisdom Project, Occupy Wall Street, Black Lives Matter, and Standing Rock for showing us the way to re-imagine our world.

About the Author

Theodore Richards is the director and founder of The Chicago Wisdom Project, a core faculty member of The Fox Institute, and the author of several books. He is the recipient of numerous literary awards, including two Independent Publisher Awards and the Nautilus Book Award. He lives in Chicago with his wife and daughters.

For more information go to his website
www.theodorerichards.com

HOMEBOUND
PUBLICATIONS

Ensuring that the mainstream isn't the only stream.

At Homebound Publications, we publish books written by independent voices for independent minds. Our books focus on a return to simplicity and balance, connection to the earth and each other, and the search for meaning and authenticity. Founded in 2011, Homebound Publications is one of the rising independent publishers in the country. Collectively through our imprints, we publish between fifteen to twenty offerings each year. Our authors have received dozens of awards, including: *Foreword Reviews'* Book of the Year, Nautilus Book Award, Benjamin Franklin Book Awards, and Saltire Literary Awards. Highly-respected among bookstores, readers and authors alike, Homebound Publications has a proven devotion to quality, originality and integrity.

We are a small press with big ideas. As an independent publisher we strive to ensure that the mainstream is not the only stream. It is our intention at Homebound Publications to preserve contemplative storytelling. We publish full-length introspective works of creative non-fiction as well as essay collections, travel writing, poetry, and novels. In all our titles, our intention is to introduce new perspectives that will directly aid humankind in the trials we face at present as a global village.

WWW.HOMEBOUNDPUBLICATIONS.COM